SPACE MATTERS

Use the wisdom of vastu to create a healthy home. 11 top designers show you how.

SPACE MATTERS

Use the wisdom of vastu to create a healthy home. 11 top designers show you how.

Kathleen Cox

Stewart, Tabori & Chang · New York

Published in 2007 by Stewart, Tabori & Chang
An imprint of Harry N. Abrams, Inc.

Text copyright © 2007 by Kathleen Cox

Library of Congress Cataloging-in-Publication Data
Cox, Kathleen.
      Space matters : use the wisdom of vastu to create
      a healthy home. 11 top designers show you how. /
by Kathleen Cox.
        p. cm.
      ISBN-13: 978-1-58479-639-8 (hardcover with jacket)
      ISBN-10: 1-58479-639-1
      1. Interior decoration–Psychological aspects.
      2. Personal
space–Psychological aspects. 3. Vastu. I. Title.

NK2113.C69 2007
747.001'9–dc22
2006100227

Editor: Dervla Kelly
Designers: Julie Hoffer and Nancy Leonard
Production Manager: Jacquie Poirier

The text of this book was composed in Bernhard
Modern and Nobel

Printed and bound in China
10 9 8 7 6 5 4 3 2 1

harry n. abrams, inc.
a subsidiary of La Martinière Groupe

115 West 18th Street
New York, NY 10011
www.hnabooks.com

PHOTOGRAPH CREDITS:

Pages 5, 6 (top left and top right), 70, 71, 74, 75, 79,
80, 81, 82, 83: photographs © Chris Corrie; pages
6 (top middle), 40, 50, 54, 55, 56, 57, 59, 60, 61, 62,
86, 87, 88, 89, 90, 176: photographs © Noah Sheldon;
pages 6 (bottom left), 47, 93, 110, 111, 112, 113, 114, 115,
116, 117, 136, 137: photographs © Kalen Jones; pages 6
(bottom middle), 105: photographs © Kelly Lerner;
pages 6 (bottom right), 150, 157, 159: photographs
© Carol Gillum; pages 12, 64, 65, 66: photographs
© 1994 by Kevin Ireton, *Fine Homebuilding magazine*,
The Taunton Press, Inc.; pages 18, 146, 161, 163, 164,
165, 166, 167: photographs © Randall Beuth; pages 21,
24, 25, 27, 28, 29 (top left, top right and bottom right),
30, 31, 44, 45, 100 (top left): photographs © Herbert
Ascherman, Jr.; pages 29 (bottom left), 101 (top), 139,
140, 143 (top right): photographs © Kathleen Cox;
pages 34, 35: photographs © Donna Hoffner; page 37:
photograph © Michael Dobrowski; pages 46, 85, 94,
100, 101, 106, 107, 108, 109, 133: photographs ©
Catherine Wanek; pages 48, 49, 73 (top), 143 (top left
and bottom left): photographs © Gaiatecture Design
Studio; page 67: photograph © Doug Atherley; pages
72, 73 (bottom), 84, 121, 129, 142, 143 (bottom right):
photographs © Primary Color, Inc.; pages 76, 122, 134:
photographs © Christian Korab/Korab Photo; pages
77, 99, 119, 130, 131, 135, 141, 154, 155: photographs
© Daniel Aubry; pages 91, 156: photographs © Bruno
Bondanelli; pages 118, 132: photographs © Sarah
Susanka; pages 138, 151, 152, 153, 158 (top): photographs © Nick Smith; page 158 (bottom): photograph
© Lauren Malley

CONTENTS

DEDICATION

For Freddy and Frances—sweet, sweet souls

ACKNOWLEDGMENTS

Many kind and generous people contributed to the creation of this book. First, I'd like to thank my special friends who have continually supported my work: Sally Helgesen, Stanley Siegel, Reniera Wolff, Peggy Price, Kathryn Kilgore, Larry Estridge, Danny Sawh, and Bobby Hamburger—along with members of my family, Ellie Menz, and Kia and Ryan Berglund.

I am also grateful to the designers who were so generous with their time. Thank you, Clodagh, Sarah Susanka, Bruno Bondanelli, Doug Atherley, Paula Baker-LaPorte and Robert LaPorte, Kalen Jones and Susie Harrington, Kelly Lerner, Mary Gordon, Linda Spence, Kim Naylor, and the thread collective—Gita Nandan, Mark Mancuso, and Elliot Maltby. Many thanks also to their clients who graciously welcomed us into their homes for photo shoots.

And this leads to ample thanks to the photographers—the amazing Daniel Aubry, Noah Sheldon, Chris Corrie, Carol Gillum, Catherine Wanek, Randy Beuth, Nick Smith, Lauren Malley, Giorgio Bracaglia, Christian Korab, Herb Ascherman, and even some of the designers who proved their talent extends into the realm of photography.

I am equally indebted to the great people at Stewart, Tabori & Chang: my enthusiastic and wise editor Dervla Kelly and the talented Julie Hoffer and Nancy Leonard who led the design team, and Marisa Bulzone who believed in my proposal and generated the interest in my work at this wonderful publishing house. Lastly, I want to thank my dear agent, Anna Ghosh. I appreciate your perseverance, nurturing spirit, and willingness to go that extra mile.

INTRODUCTION
Space Matters, and So Do the Matters of Space

We have lost sight of the meaning of that special place we call home. We have lost sight of its absolute power to influence the way we feel, day in and day out. We have also lost sight of the interrelated nature of the words in the phrase "body, mind, and soul." These three words are often used glibly—when the truth is that, in effect, they control our well-being.

The modern world encourages rapid movement and quick decision making. But when these decisions affect the home, it is necessary to do just the opposite: slow down, take time to think before settling on plans for a new home or a renovation for an old home. We should carefully evaluate every step of the process that controls the look of this important place in our lives because each design decision, individually and collectively, influences not only the quality of the home but the quality of our lives.

These days, time is so precious, and we spend much of that precious time in this one space. It ought to serve us well, make us feel good, and protect the core of our essence—our soul.

But for far too many of us, the meaning of the home has become obscured. It has come to mean many other things that get in the way of what matters. This is why I have written the book that you are holding now. I want to restore the old-fashioned meaning of home to help us all rediscover the power of this sublimely critical space.

In the 1980s, I was privileged to learn about vastu, an ancient design science connected to an unwavering holistic philosophy. This discovery enabled me to see how space really does matter. It matters as much as each one of us matters, as much as every life form—from the grass on a knoll to the animals in the forests.

I wrote two books on this design science, *Vastu Living* (Marlowe, 2000) and *the Power of Vastu Living* (Atria, 2002). And I began giving talks around the country to designers and architects and a long list of different organizations that were intrigued by what I had written. I gave individual consultations to hundreds of people who felt something was not working in their lives and hoped that I could help.

I never promised to change their lives, but I did show them that the way homes are created matters because it influences how people feel and even how they think about themselves. When clients took my words and suggestions to heart, they rediscovered the meaning of their home—and what really mattered.

In *Space Matters*, I share with you what I told them. . . .

Has it ever occurred to you that space, meaning specifically any built environment from a man-made structure to a forest glen created by nature, has a measurable impact on your well-being? Every space you enter or walk through has power, and you always react to that power. Some environments make you feel good; some make you feel nervous or uncomfortable. Other spaces may have no discernable effect, but their neutrality, in itself, reflects a power that your body notices and feels.

Just as space matters in a critical and fundamental way, so do the matters connected to space, such as lighting and color, furnishings and their arrangement, and all the other design elements that define the décor in a home. Yet few of us understand the power of space or know how to use it to our advantage.

Let me paint a picture—one that may seem familiar. You are looking through a home décor magazine, and a picture of a living room grabs your attention. You think, *Oh, what a perfect room!* You examine the details—the color of the walls, the choice of window treatments and furnishings, the objects on the shelves and tables, the artwork and photographs on the walls.

You wonder, *How can I create this same effect in my own living room?* (Which, if you had to admit it, may feel more like a dead room.)

We all want to have a calming bedroom, a comfortable living room, a well-organized kitchen that makes us feel like cooking—or, at the very least, a kitchen that makes us want to sit down at the table and eat a relaxed meal instead of standing up and eating on the go. But far too many of us believe that only great designers and those lucky few nonprofessionals born with talent get to realize this dream.

Successful design is not a result of luck. It comes from understanding how to turn the power inherent in every space to the positive. Throughout *Space Matters*, you will see the results of this awareness expressed in the appealing work of eleven thoughtful designers and architects, in collaboration with their clients.

A few of these interiors are, admittedly, fancy and had a correspondingly fancy budget. But many are not lavish and unduly expensive. They reveal a wide range of décors, from modern or Victorian to country rustic or eclectic, and an equally wide array of interior environments—from lofts, apartments, and houses to bungalows and cottages in different parts of America and England.

In every image you will see that good design is the result of purposeful intention. Each designer or architect has factored in the predictable consequences of every decision so that the power of space creates a positive impact on the people who enter these homes. The rooms connect to their owners in a deeply satisfying way and is never a result of chance.

Some of these architects and designers may be familiar to you. The architect and author Sarah Susanka has inspired countless people to rethink the appropriateness of the "McMansion" with her series of books that began with *The Not So Big House* (Taunton, 2001). The widely respected designer Clodagh wrote *Total Design* (Clarkson Potter, 2001), and her powerful interiors have been showcased in many other books.

Other architects and designers selected for *Space Matters* may be unfamiliar to you, but all these talented people and their works deserve our attention. The majority express their awareness of the positive power of nature through a commitment to green design. Some are also dedicated to the revival of traditional construction methods such as clay, straw, and timber homes, and straw bale homes.

In 2005, *Natural Home* magazine named the top ten green architects in America. The list included Santa Fe's Paula Baker-Laporte, who, along with her husband, the builder/educator Robert Laporte, founded EcoNest, and Kelly Lerner of Spokane, Washington, who founded One World Design. Mary Gordon, the founder of Gaiatecture Design Studio, based in rural western New York, and Susie Harrington and Kalen Jones, who created With Gaia Design, which operates out of Moab, Utah, are making their own green marks on two radically different American landscapes.

thread collective, a New York City architectural firm founded by Gita Nandan, Mark Mancuso, and Elliot Maltby, and Kim Nadel's NICHE environmentally smart design group, also based in New York City, were featured in New York's popular *Time Out* magazine for their commitment to green design in a city that has been called a concrete jungle. Bruno Bondanelli, a talented architect from Italy, created Designx, a company that has established a thoughtful green presence in the celluloid world of Hollywood and Los Angeles. Northward, near San Francisco, Linda Spence, founder of L. Y. Spence Designs, is an up-and-coming designer who is beginning to make her mark with her serene interiors. And Doug Atherley, who founded Kinari Design in London, celebrates the positive power of space in understated yet robust environments on both sides of the Atlantic. By examining the work of these visionaries, you will see how they design by intention and create appealing homes.

Space Matters will also enrich your understanding of the power of space by introducing you to vastu, which originated in what is now India. It is a sister science of yoga, as well as ayurveda, the science of well-being and longevity popularized in the West by Deepak Chopra. These three spiritual sciences share the same goal—to increase our well-being. The three core principles of vastu, in particular, are dedicated to designing homes so that they honor our very essence. In every respect, vastu homes *intentionally* appeal to the needs and preferences of the human body.

As you read *Space Matters*, I will also pose a series of questions intended to help you analyze your home and test your positive use of the power of space. It is my hope that these questions will help you shift the way you think about your home—so many of us have lost sight of its importance.

In this trying time of stress and fear, we need to reconnect the home to the hearth. *Hearth* is such a lovely word—sweetly encompassing the word *heart*. Yet it is rarely used these days. It is disappearing along with the fireplace.

We need our home to become our hearth again—to welcome us wholeheartedly when we step across the threshold. A home should celebrate who we are and what we love. It should be a dependable oasis. If you closely examine most of the living rooms and bedrooms and kitchens featured in magazines, you will see that the majority have one thing in common—they project cohesion and calm. They do not look like rooms that generate stress.

Like Dorothy, who was whisked away by a tornado to the land of Oz, we've been whisked away, too. We need to accept the truth—that in properly designed spaces there really is—or really should be—no place like home. Home, sweet home.

We create a home with our heart and our soul. They tell us how to proceed.
Our heart and our soul take the lead in design, not our eyes.

CHAPTER ONE:
Design to Please the Human Body

We all want our house or apartment to be welcoming and appealing—a place where we love to be. Yet for many of us, that dream home remains elusive. When forced to make a decision about décor, we struggle to articulate what we want and end up speaking in vague terms about preferring this color or that, this style of sofa or that type of window treatment. Most of us get rattled because we try to identify our needs solely in terms of the visual—we tend to think with our eyes.

Yes, it is perfectly appropriate to long for an attractive home, but this should be merely one part of the objective. The successfully designed home does much more than please the eye. The ideal home is *viscerally* appealing. It satisfies emotionally and physically, even spiritually.

So how to create this place? First, it is necessary to identify the underlying yet tangible feelings associated with the home. We need to think about what *home* means to us and what we want it to do. Only then is it possible to fully appreciate the extraordinary importance of this special place.

We also need to understand the inherent power connected to every space surrounding us. A home can make us feel good, or out of sorts. It has a direct bearing on our state of well-being. And because space is so inherently powerful, it's important to learn to use it effectively to create a place that connects to us, deeply.

What Is the Home?

The dictionary defines *home* as a residence, a physical structure in which people live, or a shelter that protects them. But these descriptions seem more appropriate for the word *house*. When I think of a house, I see, in particular, the physical structure—remember that drawing so many of us create as children that showed a house with a leafy tree in a grassy yard and a circular sun ablaze in the sky? The image that comes to me is external, the physical shelter with a roof and outer walls and a big front door.

When I think of a home, however, I see a collection of interiors—the backdrops for the intimate tableaux that unfold inside a private world. I imagine a family at a kitchen table enjoying a meal, children playing in a bedroom, a couple sitting together in a living room. I see personal, unguarded moments that represent domestic life.

I also see the home as one place that continues to be under our personal control. We can legitimately consider our home, however small or modest, as a castle where we are in charge. We decide how to furnish the rooms, who comes inside, who breaks bread with us, and who can share an evening or spend a weekend or a month with us. The rules and rituals established by a home's inhabitants create a predictable and comforting set of rhythms with special meaning.

One house may be physically identical to another in the neighborhood, or an apart-ment or loft may be built on the same plan as another unit in the building. But once these copycat structures are furnished, each feels different inside. In a successful home, the décor expresses the personalities and needs of its occupants.

Many homes fail to do this. I see this firsthand when I visit clients. They know something is not working in their apartment or house—and invariably they are right. Most homes that I analyze are so impersonal, or the inhabitants have retreated so far into the world of neutral, that the rooms express nothing about them as individuals. These failed homes suffer from what I call a "décor of disconnect."

The Power of Space

There is power attached to every space we enter, yet few of us make conscious note of it. So let's take a moment to experience this through an analysis of two different environ-ments. Think of the last time you walked down a dimly lit public stairwell or sat cramped in the tight quarters of an airplane. Remember how you felt about that experience? Most likely, you couldn't wait to escape the unap-pealing environment.

Those are examples of negative spaces, and they illustrate the influence of space on our well-being. Negative space typically drags us down and sets our nerves on edge. Some spaces actually induce a state of fear and activate the fight-or-flight mechanism. Our adrenal glands pump hormones through

ABOVE: Negative space.

RIGHT: Positive space.

the body, creating a heightened state of alert. Our blood pressure shoots up, our heart rate accelerates. At such times, we suffer from all the symptoms associated with acute stress. Of course, this is an extreme response to an extremely negative space, but all negative spaces create a feeling of unease and can contribute to chronic stress, which is surely not healthy. Notice what happens to you the next time that you enter an unappealing space. Your body probably stiffens or you emotionally withdraw. You are exhibiting signs of stress, however small the dose.

Now imagine taking a quiet stroll along a sandy stretch of beach as the sun sets on a summer day. Vibrant colors spread across the sky just above the horizon. Shimmering sunrays ripple on the surface of the darkening water. You delight in the sounds of the calling seagulls and the rhythmic pounding of the waves that roll up on the sand and erase your footprints.

During such an idyllic walk, the body tends to release its tension. You become so aware of your connection to the natural world around you that you feel intrinsically at one with this sympathetic environment. This calming stretch of beach is an example of a positive space. Instead of compelling us to withdraw, it invites us to turn inward. We may grow so still that we can hear that quiet yet loyal inner voice that celebrates our individuality and absolute worth.

There are also neutral spaces, which are purposely made so inoffensive that, in effect, their power is ignored. Many hotel environments, especially lobbies, may be visually impressive, with marble, brass, and a fancy atrium. Yet these environments are generally emotionally and spiritually empty. They are designed as transient, neutral spaces, attractive but unwelcoming. We're not supposed to linger; the management prefers that we simply pass through. And since neutral space fails to take advantage of positive power a neutral space does nothing to boost our well-being. It is a negative space in disguise. Only a positive space works its magic on us.

Unclaimed Space

In today's tight real-estate market, people can struggle for months to find a home that meets their list of critical requirements—acceptable price, acceptable number and size and layout of rooms, acceptable location in a community. For a lot of people, this search ends with an unwanted compromise. They sign their new deed or lease feeling that they have settled for second best or worse, so their mind sows the seeds of discontent. They immediately envision themselves living somewhere else.

As soon as these people move into their imperfect house or apartment, they talk in disparaging terms about the new space, or they make apologies for it. And they never refer to it as home. It is their house or their apartment or "my place." They may even leave a few boxes unpacked—piled up in a closet or stacked against a wall. But these

ABOVE: Neutral space.

unopened boxes, even if they are out of sight, are never out of mind. Their message makes a clear statement: "I refuse to claim this place as my own space and turn it into my home."

Until we claim personal place as our own space, however, we can't create a meaningful home. Living in a state of unrelieved transition, we remain preoccupied with the past or the future. This is unsettling—physically, emotionally, and mentally.

Claiming personal space, flaws and all, is the necessary first step toward the creation of a successful home. Unless we take this action, a house or apartment will continue to resemble the worst aspects of a hotel suite. It feels like an impersonal stopover. But it is only masquerading as a hotel suite—it lacks the hotel housekeeper. Invariably, when a place remains unclaimed, it isn't taken care of, either. The negativity attached to the perception of that space slowly attaches to its inhabitants and damages the soul.

But how can we shake off passivity and actively begin the process of turning negative space into positive?

We can draw on the insights of vastu. The theories expressed in this science will refresh our understanding of the importance of home and help shift the way we think about space. We will acquire a clearer understanding of our innate response to design and learn how to create a special home that offers calm and tranquility in this complicatedly wired and always-on world.

Introducing Vastu

Vastu originated in the Indian subcontinent during the time of the Vedic culture, which flourished more than 5,000 years ago. To this day, the people of India modestly call vastu their science of architecture and design. But it is not merely about design aesthetics. It is about the nature of the universe and our relationship to it. Specifically, vastu is based on the Vedic idea that harmony within and without comes from observing the proper relationship with every space one inhabits. Simply put, vastu's ancient scholars believed that before internal peace can be achieved, a person must find external peace. To this end, they created a design science to help restore balance and well-being by creating a healthy and soothing home environment.

Along with yoga and ayurveda, which share the same philosophy, vastu makes up the Vedic mind-body-soul equation. All three sciences aim to increase emotional, physical, and spiritual well-being. While yoga and ayurveda focus on the body, vastu focuses on the surrounding environments.

Vastu is the critical outer layer in this wellness triangle—because living in an environment that undermines well-being will end up undermining the benefits that come from good exercise and healthy eating. Only recently have Western scientists and psychologists begun to study and acknowledge what the Vedic scholars understood: that the surrounding environment influences health.

Think about the 1990s phenomenon of the McMansion, the mega house that often looks shoehorned into its too-small footprint. Inside the customary grand entryway, with its typical two-story vaulted ceiling, the scale is off between the supersized dwelling and the human form. The McMansion is all about volume. It is a house, not a home. A real home never makes us feel small.

Is there an area in your home that is a source of discomfort? Many of us instinctively steer clear of those problem spaces. We race through or even circle around them. But that only turns negative space into wasted or abandoned space. Given the high cost of housing, abandoning a space is an expensive way to cope with a negative space.

Think about any space that you avoid in your home. List the reasons why you think you keep away from it. Dig deep. Consider how you respond to the space, emotionally and physically. Your reasons probably connect to more than the color on the walls or the fabric on a chair.

ABOVE: Contemporary McMansion.

RIGHT: Appropriately proportioned house.

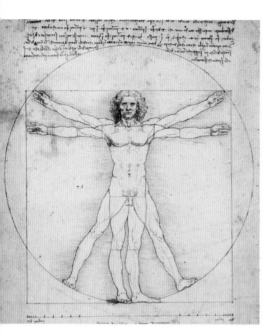

Pleasing the Human Body

The Vedic scholars, who understood the basic human need for harmony and balance, determined that vastu would deliberately use the human body as the guiding force in the creation of any man-made structure. Observing the principle that the best architecture respects the body's own magnificent architecture in proportion and in form, they saw that when people create spaces that honor the human body, they humanize those places—a concept that is too often undervalued in today's stressful world.

In the first century B.C.E., the Roman architect and engineer Marcus Vitruvius Pollio wrote the ten-volume *De Architectura*, or *On Architecture*, the world's oldest surviving work on this subject. In it, he describes the aesthetic principles and proportions expressed in classical Greek design. The third volume compares architecture to the human form and inspired Leonardo da Vinci's drawing of the Vitruvian man.

Vitruvius noted that the body's length and breadth, measured from the top of the head to the soles of the feet and from the tips of the fingers of each outstretched arm, are roughly equal. The human form creates a square, with the navel at the center.

But long before the advent of the Roman Empire and the birth of Vitruvius and da Vinci, the Vedic scholars had already made a similar observation. These scholars concluded that of all the existing shapes, including circles and triangles, the square, with its four equal and symmetrical sides, existed as the most perfect form. They used the square to symbolize their view of the universe, the harmony and balance that they ascribed to the heavenly realm. In their view, it was fitting that the orderly balance of the square would be mirrored in the ideal human form.

The Vedic scholars went on to observe that, despite its overall symmetry, most of the body's features, such as eyes, ears, hands, feet, and breasts, are actually slightly asymmetrical. Examine your face in a mirror. Notice the shape of your eyebrows, the size and shape of your eyes, and the thickness and curve of your lips. Hold out your hands and look at the lengths and the taper of each set of fingers. Are your two hands identical? Look down at your bare feet. Are they perfectly symmetrical? Most likely not.

As was customary with Vedic scholars, they looked beyond the human form and studied the surrounding environment. They analyzed the shapes of the trees, the flowers, everything that existed in the natural world. They noted that what is true about the human body is true within the world of nature. Nearly every created form, from a rock and a leaf to the shape of a lake, is asymmetrical. Even a single blade of grass exhibits an asymmetrical contour.

Over time, the Vedic scholars incorporated their observations about the human body and the power of space into a sophisticated system of design. *Vastu* is a Sanskrit word that means "created or built space," or "dwelling site." They intended for each meaning attached to the word to extend to the human body.

Few people think of the body as an example of built space, but it is. The body is created by the union of egg and sperm. Our body is also a dwelling site: It shelters the inner being or soul. In sum, it is a perfect example of vastu—and a perfect example of living architecture.

Everything that exists is an example of vastu: each and every man-made structure (again, this includes human beings), each and every unique expression of flora and fauna, and each and every aspect of the universe, which reaches beyond our vision and imagination. And since these ancient scholars were constantly incorporating their theories into the heart of a spiritual philosophy that honors all creation, they made another meaningful connection. They concluded that all existence is interrelated and interdependent, from an unnamed star to an organism living unseen at the bottom of the ocean. Nothing in the grand universal scheme exists in isolation, and everything that exists serves a valuable purpose and function. Even the intended design of each created object follows this rule. The scholars were certain that the color, shape, texture, and size of every object adhered to a predetermined pattern that maintains order in the universe.

On one level, this theory is an expression of contemporary holism, but in the ancient Vedic texts and vastu, it assumed a spiritual dimension. The philosophy that flows through vastu includes the principle that we must respect and preserve all creation. Everything that exists is divine.

As with pearls strung on a necklace, if the fragile string breaks, the entire necklace unravels. So it is with every aspect of the created world. If one piece is damaged, all creation will be damaged as a result. This belief represents the Vedic law of nature. The ancient scholars believed that there is nothing random in creation; everything has an absolute value; everything matters in the profound design and scheme of the universe. And they were certain that upsetting the law of nature would upset the intrinsic order of the universe.

Today, global warming appears to validate their ideas. The gradual warming of the climate is melting the huge glaciers and ice caps in the polar regions. This process, in turn, is causing a rise in sea levels that will threaten coastal areas. Droughts are on the increase; hurricanes are more severe. This chain reaction is disturbing the earth's harmony and balance—and, as the ancient scholars asserted, all creation will endure the consequences.

The Vedic law of nature is the fundamental

LEFT: DaVinci's *Vitruvian Man*.

ABOVE: Body equals a square.

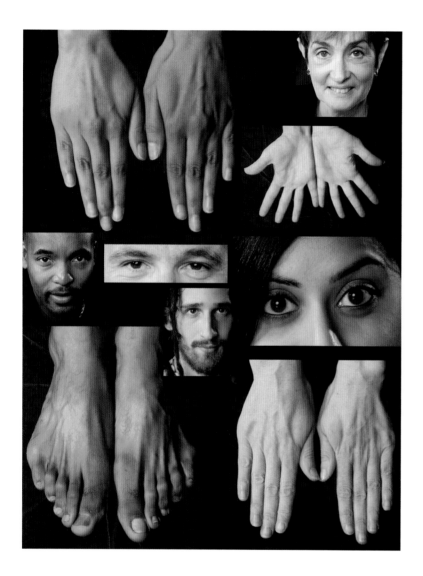

ABOVE: Our asymmetric features.

RIGHT: Asymmetry in nature.

rule in vastu, and the Vedic scholars held that every dwelling should observe this law to ensure the well-being of its occupants. When the design of a space honors the needs and preferences of the individuals who live there—this includes the needs and preferences of the human body—the environment makes positive use of its inherent power. Harmony prevails.

The Three Core Principles of Vastu

The essential theories in vastu revolve around three core principles:

1. The need to align our biorhythms with the universal rhythms, in which the sun plays the most important role.

2. The need to respect our interconnection with nature and welcome it into the home.

3. The need to celebrate who we are and what we love in every space so that we create supportive environments.

Let's look at each of these principles and see how they work together to create a healthy, inspirational home.

ALIGNING BIORHYTHMS WITH THE SUN

The Vedic scholars had a remarkable understanding of the primary planets in the solar system. They understood that the earth was not flat but round. They figured out that it revolved around the sun long before the Greek mathematician Pythagoras, who lived about 500 B.C.E., and the sixteenth-century astronomer Nicolaus Copernicus. Thousands of years before Newton, they developed theories about the law of gravity and other notions about physics that predate the works of Western scholars.

They also understood how gravitational forces knit the solar system together and affect this planet. They noticed, in particular, the ongoing rhythms in the rotation of the moon around the earth and in the rotation of the earth around the sun. They realized that these orbits lead to the orderly expression of time and passage of the seasons. They observed the rhythmic patterns of the changing climate and weather.

In addition, Vedic scholars had a sophisticated understanding of the human body. Ayurveda, the Vedic science of longevity and wellness, is the earliest known form of health care to focus on disease prevention. Its body of wisdom, which is as old as the wisdom that supports vastu, reveals an extraordinary comprehension of the biological systems at work within the human body.

Drawing upon their knowledge of the solar system, the practitioners of ayurveda reasoned that the rhythms associated with the sun and moon influenced the body's rhythms and, for that matter, the rhythms that exist within all living organisms. They saw that the

rupted. He feels irritable, tired; he suffers from poor concentration and decreased motor control. Even his digestive system feels out of whack.

Who hasn't fallen victim to a case of the blahs after staying up late on weekend nights and sleeping a bit longer the morning after? The internal clock falls behind and disrupts the body's natural rhythms. Going back to work on Monday morning, we are not only tired, but suffering from the Monday morning blues.

All life forms, from animals and birds to tiny fruit flies and microscopic bacteria and fungi, have biorhythms, which scientists now call circadian rhythms. *Circadian* comes from two Latin words: *circa*, meaning "about," and *dies*, meaning "day." "About a day" aptly describes the duration of a complete cycle, which lasts twenty-four to twenty-five hours.

The circadian rhythm not only controls the sleep-wake cycle and many daily activities, but also most physiological functions. Think about the process of breathing: the steady stretching and constricting of the lungs, the ongoing pumping of oxygen through the blood, and the rhythmic beating of the heart. The minute you bite a piece of food, you trigger yet another series of internal rhythms connected to the metabolic and digestive system: swallowing the food, burning calories to produce energy, and passing the remaining waste through the intestinal tract. Circadian rhythm affects cell proliferation, hormonal

extent to which all these rhythms work together, undisturbed and undisrupted, benefits the health of each life form. Western scientists have started to research and validate some of the ancient scholars' ideas in the relatively new field of science called chronobiology, which studies the effects of time and rhythm on living organisms.

The body is such a subtle machine that it is easy to overlook the way that it works until it goes off kilter. A business woman boards an airplane and travels through time zones. After a six-hour flight from west to east, she gets off the plane in time for breakfast. But her internal clock is saying that it's 3:00 a.m.—that she should be asleep in bed.

Or a computer technician finds himself working the night shift. And no matter how many hours he sleeps during the day, he cannot catch up. His internal clock is dis-

production, and many transmissions from the motor and sensory neurons that pulse back and forth to the brain by way of the nervous system.

Scientists now know this elaborate system of rhythms is continually reset by external cues such as the outside temperature (since it is warmer by day and cooler by night) and the presence of light or darkness. They call these external cues *zeitgebers*, a German word for "time-givers." An alarm clock could be considered a zeitgeber, though, of course, an artificial one.

Most scientists believe that the sun is the dominant zeitgeber and that the rhythmic alternation of sunlight and darkness has a significant impact on our health. Study after study shows that humans, by nature, are designed to be diurnal creatures. Most of us feel best working by day and sleeping by night. One recent study has even shown that infants, start to shift their sleep pattern to the nighttime to synchronize their internal clock within three days of being born. Even at this tender age, the human body wants to get itself on a healthy daytime-nighttime schedule.

All these scientific conclusions validate the theories of the Vedic scholars. And these scholars studied more than these rhythms and how they functioned. They studied the quality of the sun's rays—or just the presence of the light—and observed that it changes during the course of the day.

The early-morning sun, they noted, is a source of calm and rejuvenation, while the midday and afternoon sun can be intense and exhausting. This explains why yogis in India traditionally faced the northeast and the rising sun when they practiced their yoga and meditated. They wanted to absorb this light, with its restorative powers. The light's physically calming quality also mirrored the state of the yogic mind and spirit when they did their postures and settled into meditation.

It is possible to see the difference between morning light and evening light. Compare the colors that appear in a typical sunrise and sunset. The early rays that accompany the dawn on a storm-free day bring a ripple of soft pastels of pink and yellow, along with metallic hues of gold and silver. In the evening, the sun, as it slides beneath the

LEFT: Sunrise.

ABOVE: Sunset.

horizon, often leaves in a blaze of color—fiery hues of red and orange or vivid magenta, or bright yellow hues streaked with deep gold. The intense colors seem to bleed through the darkening sky.

Environmentalists have noted that particles of dust, smog, and smoke, which are caused by human activity, slowly rise in the atmosphere during the course of the day. At dusk, this accumulation of particles contributes to the sunset's colorful intensity. Some of these particles dissipate during the night, so the sun rises in a partially cleansed sky. It is ironic to think that pollution contributes to the beauty attributed to a sunset; but, to some degree, this is true, and this phenomenon helps explains why the sunrise feels so calming. Its gentle light is more pure and less sullied.

For years, so many people have followed medical warnings and covered their skin with sunblock before stepping into the light of day, whether it's sunny or cloudy. But now medical researchers assert that modest exposure to direct sunlight, especially in the morning, is beneficial. Ultraviolet rays from the sun activate the process in the body that creates vitamin D, which strengthens bones and helps fight problems such as hypertension, heart disease, diabetes, and depression. Vitamin D may even ward off some forms of cancer. Recent studies have also shown that when babies receive small daily doses of sunlight,

they sleep better at night; other studies reveal that lack of sunlight contributes to sleep deprivation, which may explain why many adults who work in windowless rooms have trouble sleeping.

So how do Vedic theories about the healing nature of morning sunlight influence the first vastu principle, which encourages the alignment of the body's rhythms with the sun's rhythms? Vedic scholars determined that a healthy home provides for ample exposure to revitalizing morning light and limited exposure to strong afternoon light, which makes us unnaturally tired. We all know how the intense sun at this time of the day can make us sleepy when it pours into a room, especially in the summer.

In the practice of vastu in the Northern Hemisphere, this principle leads to the placement of low, delicate, and light-weight furnishings in the north and east of a room so that the morning sun streams unrestricted through the windows. Heavier and taller furnishings are placed in the south and west to form a barrier against harmful midday and afternoon rays. (In the Southern Hemisphere, lightweight and delicate furnishings would be placed in the south and east, and bulky, tall furnishings in the north and west.)

Centuries ago, furniture placement was the most effective solution for controlling exposure to the sun inside the house. Today there are sophisticated solar treatments, such as window films that are more effective at regulating the presence of the sun in our home. Nonetheless, vastu practitioners continue to observe this principle of alignment—even if there are no windows in the north or the east. Why is this? By establishing this level of mindfulness in the orientation of furnishings, they honor their relationship with the sun, even in its absence. Equally important, this placement introduces and reinforces the power of asymmetry, which appeals to the human body. Our body instinctively relaxes in asymmetrically organized rooms, as you will learn.

We benefit in one other way from this asymmetric layout. Generally, Western design is symmetric, and symmetry puts the focus of a room in the center of the wall. But when we design asymmetrically, our focus shifts to the room's four corners. This focus, which makes us notice the diagonal distance inside a room, makes the interior feel larger and more spacious.

Finally, the vastu layout, when repeated from room to room, creates cohesion. Every room becomes part of a unified whole. And this cohesion, a subtle expression of holism, is spiritually comforting and reassuring.

BRINGING NATURE INTO THE HOME

Vastu's second principle asks us to revere nature and liberally incorporate it into our interior décor. Most of us revere nature outside the home. We eagerly embrace ecology and holism—and support the need to ensure the planet's survival. We work hard to do our part so that we don't become part of the problem. Most of us even understand the taxing issue of non-biodegradable products, which linger forever and, in many cases, injure the earth. We act on our concerns; we do our best to protect our environment.

But too often many of us fail to extend this belief to our own oneness with everything else and protect ourselves from harm. We bring toxins that harm the natural environment into our interior environments. An inventory of the products in a typical home, from the particle board that goes into the construction of so much furniture to the toxin-laden paints that cover the walls, would reveal that the practice of holism often stops at the front door.

Yet natural products are so often appealing to the senses, including the sense of touch. Hold a plastic bottle or Styrofoam cup—then hold a leaf, a wicker basket, a seashell, a handful of sand, or any glass object (which is made of sand). Nature, unlike plastic, registers with our senses. We respond favorably to organic products, which come from the earth. Their presence in the home honors our symbiotic connection, interconnection, and interdependence with all that exists. Nature nurtures; the power of our relationship with nature gives us an emotional, spiritual, and physical lift.

ABOVE: Before vastu.

RIGHT: After vastu.

CELEBRATING WHO WE ARE AND WHAT WE LOVE

The third vastu principle is a reminder to respect our unique nature—our special essence—and the special essence of anyone who may share our home. We show this respect by mindfully creating a décor in our home that unquestionably honors who we are and what we love.

The artwork and photographs on the walls of each room reflect this, as do the objects on the tables and the shelves; everything in our home reflects our identity and what we love. Entering any space in a personalized home triggers a visceral, positive response. We instinctively relax and feel at home. This is a critical difference between an authentic home and a house or an apartment. The former welcomes us; the latter, with its décor of disconnect, doesn't speak to us at all.

SEE WHAT HAPPENS!

A homeowner in Hudson Valley, New York was unhappy with the northwestern part of her living room. Her furnishings fit into the space; but the area didn't feel or look right to her.

See what happens when she reorganized the space according to vastu's three principles.

Principle One—aligning our biorhythms with the rhythms of the sun:
She removed the bulky cabinet that was in the north of the room and replaced it with a

delicate, lightweight table. The window, with its gentle northern light and outside view of trees, became a calming point of focus.

Principle Two—welcoming nature into the home:

She placed a potted plant on the floor by the window and added the table with its natural finish that echoed the patina of the flooring. She brought the outside inside and celebrated the healing power of nature.

Principle Three—celebrating who we are and what we love:

She honored herself in this part of the room. She showcased objects on the wall and on the table that reflected her tastes, loves, and preferences. By creating an asymmetric placement with the scroll elevated to the left of the table, she created flow: our eyes gently move toward the right and take in the painting and the plant on the floor. She repeated this same flow with her asymmetric placement of the statues on the table: the tallest carving on the left guides our eyes toward the shorter statues.

By observing vastu's three principles, the homeowner successfully turned a problematic part of her living room into a calming oasis. She didn't spend money; she simply rearranged some furnishings and paid attention to the vastu goal in design: to create spaces so that they appeal to the body and the mind. This is how we create healthy interiors.

Space Matters, and So Do the Matters of Space

Once we realize that all created space has the power to influence our well-being, we are ready to learn to use this power to healthy advantage and create a home that satisfies our needs. In the following chapters, you will learn about the critical matters connected to space, from lighting and use of color to the choice and arrangement of special objects in the home. The work of successful architects and designers will demonstrate how these professionals use such critical matters to create appealing environments.

Through their example and through a shift in ways of thinking about design, you will see that design questions that once left you confused and frustrated are easy to resolve. You will see how your visceral reaction to a space consistently enables you to make the appropriate decisions governing its décor. You have the power to create the home of your dreams, where you will feel secure, reinforced, and honored. This is a worthy and *attainable* goal.

RIGHT: Vastu-designed bedroom.

WHAT DOES HOME MEAN TO YOU?

"For me, home is a sanctuary. It is a place that is sparse yet balanced, simple yet elegant—a place where I can truly be myself."
—BRUNO BONDANELLI, DESIGNX

"Home is the place that reflects who we are, who we want to become, and where we've come from."
—KIM NADEL, NICHE ENVIRONMENTALLY SMART DESIGN GROUP

"Home is where I ground myself. It is a place, any place, where I can let go and feel comfortable."
—CLODAGH, CLODAGH DESIGN

"Home is my sanctuary—it's my creative generator. Most of my good ideas come out of being silent inside my home. This is where I meditate, and these meditations become the little kernels that turn into the physical buildings around me."
—ROBERT LAPORTE, ECONEST

"Bau-biologie, which is the German study of built environments, talks about the home as our third skin. My home is an extension and expression of me, a place of my own in the world. It houses my soul, and it is the place I share with the ones I love."
—PAULA BAKER-LAPORTE, ECONEST

"Home touches my soul the way no other place does. It evokes within me a deep and profoundly intimate relationship between me and the space and life's experiences. And I feel when this connection occurs, for any of us, the home becomes the direct extension of our intellect, spirit, and physical body."
—MARY GORDON, GAIATECTURE DESIGN STUDIO

"Home means family and relaxation. While I could never live in a show home, I do need a calm and uncluttered space to shut out city life. Of course, this is not always possible with a two-year-old son!"
—DOUG ATHERLEY, KINARI DESIGN

"Ideally, a home doesn't just shelter us but allows us to flourish in comfortable spaces that are well designed for our needs, activities, and possessions. For us, the landscape is an integral part of home. This is where we get to know and interact with the plants, birds, bugs, and weather. Having this sense of connection naturally translates into a desire for our home to have as little harmful impact on the environment as possible."

–SUSIE HARRINGTON AND KALEN JONES, WITH GAIA DESIGN

"To me, home means 'the center.' It's a gathering place for family and friends, a place to nurture and be nurtured with food, rest, companionship, and the everyday rhythms of nature. Time at home restores my vitality and my creativity."

–KELLY LERNER, ONE WORLD DESIGN

"Home is about nature and nurture. And I believe the most welcoming homes embrace both nature and the individualism that nurtures homeowners. Homes contain our most personal expressions and should create comfort and ease for living. That's what my home is about."

–LINDA SPENCE OF L. Y. SPENCE DESIGNS

"My home is my sanctuary. It's the place where I center myself, and it is the source of a large part of my inspiration. It reflects me to myself."

–SARAH SUSANKA, SUSANKA STUDIOS

"We often think of the home as a physical place that evokes certain feelings. But I think less about the place and more about the sensation: We can be at home in many different places. Home also connects to the individual, so understanding the conditions that bring about our feeling of being 'at home' and how such sensations impact us is critical to consider when we design a home for a client."

–GITA NANDAN, thread collective

Nothing exists in absolute isolation, and everything that exists serves a valuable purpose and function. The intended design of every created object honors this rule.

CHAPTER TWO:
Function and Ambience—Match Them Up

What makes a house or an apartment feel like a home when we step inside? This is an important question, and thoughtful answers generally focus on the intended or unintended ambience—the mood generated by a space. Answering the question probably requires describing how we spend time inside the home. It might, for example, feel like home because we can relax and unwind or because we feel safe in this special place.

The power inherent in a home is conveyed through the ambience of its rooms. A person's visual reaction to a room triggers a visceral reaction, and this visceral reaction—a feeling or series of feelings—lingers long after the image of the room fades away. So it is critically important to create the appropriate ambience.

So how is this done? The founders of vastu emphasized that, before the décor for any room can be decided, its specific function must be considered. How do you plan to use the actual space?

In a successful home, function and ambience always reinforce each other. The dining room has a décor that is appropriate for dining, the bathroom has a décor that is appropriate for bathing, and the bedroom has a décor that is appropriate for sleeping and other intimate bedroom activities. Ambiguity or conflicting mixed signals are never sent from the eyes to the brain.

That probably sounds obvious. But in this age of multitasking, our habit of doing many things at once has invaded the home and left its imprint on the décor. As a result, the function designated to a specific area or room has become obscured. In many contemporary homes, order has given way to disorder.

Think about the process of multitasking, how it works and how it makes you feel. Imagine that you are trying to feed a hungry toddler, while fielding an important phone call and cooking dinner for the rest of the family. Your concentration is compromised each time you switch from task to task, and you are never completely engaged in any one of them. And they really do qualify as *tasks*—sources of stress—not special occasions that provide you with pleasure. In fact, you are probably doing every activity (task) as fast as you can to get to that future moment when you have finished everything you have to do now. What a strange way to live! It corrodes the ability to appreciate whatever we are doing at present.

It may not be possible to wriggle free from multitasking on the job (where, by the way, studies have shown that it actually reduces efficiency and productivity, and increases company costs). But in our home, where we do exert control, we should take advantage of the power to keep this unproductive habit from sneaking into our home life and décor, where it blurs or buries the function of a room. At home, no one wants to walk into a room and be confronted by reminders of how much work there is to be done or how disorganized things are.

Sometimes a muddled ambience is the result of simple and avoidable clutter. So few of us understand how to deal with it effectively—that subject will be addressed in Chapter Five, "Defining Details." But more often, the confusion is the result of a failure to set up a room so that its function is clear.

We must always remind ourselves that within the sanctity of the home, time is extremely precious. This precious time should be used meaningfully. But we can

Look around your kitchen. Has it become a gathering place for objects that have nothing to do with cooking and eating? Is a corner of the counter the convenient parking lot for keys, cellular phones, and mail? Has the wicker fruit basket become a catchall for unpaid bills and dry-cleaning tickets? Examine the dining room. Has your dining table turned into a home office or storage area? Do you rarely use the room for dining? An invading décor of disconnect has robbed these special rooms of their ambience and function. Over the next few days, remove objects that interfere with the function of the room. Can you feel the change in the ambience?

only do this if we remain engaged in the present moment, in whatever we are doing then and there, whether it is relaxing in a cozy chair with a good book or watching TV, taking a bath, or eating a meal with loved ones. Our surroundings should support restorative activities that release the rejuvenating power that exists in a healthy home. Visible evidence of multitasking—from unopened mail or unpaid bills that sit like ticking time bombs on the counter to the portable phones and computers—should never distract from the calming rituals legitimately connected to the function of a room. Unwittingly creating an unhealthy ambience will put us in an unhealthy frame of mind.

A décor that supports the function of the room encourages us to stay in the moment. We concentrate on the present and empty our minds of worrisome thoughts about yesterday's troubles and tomorrow's demands. In a dining room where the décor is exclusively connected to dining, the mind shifts to uplifting thoughts about the good company and the conversation to be enjoyed along with a good meal.

In a nutshell, we benefit on so many levels when the ambience of each room in a home is matched to its function. An appropriate décor keeps us grounded, and this helps reduce the day's accumulation of stress, replacing it with calm. This is an effective use of the power of space. It reinforces harmony and balance in the home and within each of us.

Multipurpose Room Versus Multitasking Décor

There is a difference between a multipurpose room and a room where the function has been sacrificed or forgotten. In a multipurpose room, the placement of furnishings carefully divides the space to make us aware of the function assigned to each area of the room. A large room can be divided into an eating area and an entertainment area and include a section designated as the home office. There are all sorts of legitimate configurations for multipurpose rooms. Each one just needs to be organized so that it is clearly defined and we feel the ambience that supports each function of the divided space.

The Three Classifications of Space Connected to the Home

Vastu divides the house or apartment into three classifications of space. Think of an idyllic setting where a house is nestled behind a picket fence with a gate that leads through a front yard to the front door.

THE TRANSITIONAL SPACE

The world on the far side of the fence belongs to the exterior world, which is usually beyond our influence and control. After opening the gate and stepping onto the property, we enter the transitional space. This space is connected to the

home. It is under the control of the home-owner and is often under the control of the renter.

The transitional space serves as a bridge connecting the exterior world outside the home to the private world inside the home. The most obvious transitional space is a front yard with an inviting front walk or a front porch that brackets the entryway. But a modest stoop also qualifies as an intermediary space that connects the public and private worlds.

How can something as nominal as a stoop, with just a few stairs, have a significance similar to a rolling lawn? It symbolically connects the outer world to the private world of the personalized home. The transitional space connected to a residence is the secular version of the threshold to a temple. When we occupy this space, we are about to enter or leave the hallowed grounds of the home, which is the temple of the body, just as the body is the temple of the soul.

Transitional spaces should invite us to linger long enough to experience a mental, emotional, and physical shift. Before entering the home, we should try to shake away all concerns associated with the external world, like shaking away dust that accumulates on our shoes. By the time we open the front door, we want to be ready to let the welcoming ambience wash over us.

The Front Yard

We who are lucky enough to have a front yard attached to our homes should do more with it than sow seeds for a lawn and plant flowers and shrubs. We should use this valuable patch of land to cultivate an ambience that reinforces the function of this important intermediary place.

But many people, especially those who live in contemporary suburbia, appear to have succumbed to a new design trend that promotes isolation and unneighborly behavior. There was a time, and it wasn't long ago, when people did more than landscape their front yard. They used it. Children played there year-round, parents sat on the front porch (front porches rarely appear on houses in new developments) or set up lawn chairs directly on grass in warm-weather months. From these vantage points, everyone could socialize with the neighbors. People would chat, trade gossip, and comment on the state of the world unfolding around them.

Back then, this daily ritual bonded the neighborhood—and it was a comforting sight. In modern-day suburbia, the front yard rarely doubles as a social setting. One long stretch of green connects property to property. The only hint of human activity comes from the cars that pass in and out of the driveways.

What happened? Why did so many of us surrender our front yards and put home life under wraps, keeping it tucked inside the house or relegated to the backyard, out of the neighbors' sight? Wouldn't it be more sensible and sociable to reclaim the front yard—and make meaningful use of that valuable transitional space?

Look at these two different transitional environments on the following pages. With each example, the homeowners have cultivated their landscape so that it flows almost seamlessly into the external world beyond their property line.

In the home designed by Susie Harrington and Kalen Jones, founders of the architectural firm With Gaia Design, the majestic, soaring buttes of southern Utah are mirrored in the rocky outcroppings jutting up near the walkway that leads to the front door. The buttes are also pleasingly mirrored in the architectural lines of the undulating roof.

The second home, in western New York, belongs to an artist and her husband, an optometrist. They have paid attention to every aspect of their personal environment from the exterior of the home, which looks so cozy against its backdrop of towering trees, to the interior, which you will see in the course of this book. The burst of flowers on either side of the walkway to the front door are neither tidy nor prim. How easy to imagine the tall spikes and bushy growth waving at us in the breeze.

Both of these homes are so welcoming. Their scale and proportion are just right. Each of them is designed to please the human body, and their transitional spaces emphasize this fact.

These two transitional spaces remind people to linger. It is easy to imagine sitting in

one of the chairs in front of the Utah home and enjoying its rugged view; in the Rochester home, the front steps and side porch provide comfortable spots where one could sit and listen to the rustle of autumn leaves or the cicadas' summer hum. These transitional spaces blend nature, which represents the outside zone, with personal choices and preferences, which reflect the private zone of the home. We willingly slow down and take time to enjoy such special, safe-feeling places. This is so important in a fear-stricken, up-tempo world, which often tells us to watch out, keep moving and doing.

We owe it to ourselves and our health to put on the brakes occasionally and coast to a halt. Transitional spaces encourage this by turning down the mental noise that yammers inside the head. They encourage us to listen instead to that quiet yet reassuring voice deep within the soul.

LEFT: Urban stoop.

ABOVE: Suburban front yards.

LEFT: Transitional environment
in Utah—idyllic by day.

RIGHT: Idyllic by night.

ABOVE: Transitional environment
in western New York.

RIGHT: Nature and the human hand.

RIGHT: Welcoming flowers.

The Foyer or Interior Entry

Even if we live in an apartment or loft we can let the foyer or interior entryway function as a transitional space. In these situations, the key is to create an ambience that matches the function of the exterior transitional space. This is not smoke and mirrors; the goal is to recreate the effect of nature inside the home.

The appealing display pictured to the left is just inside the small entryway of a loft that is home to two people who live and work in New York City, one of America's most energized and energy-sapping cities. When the couple enters the lobby of their building, they take the elevator to a neutral corridor that leads to their front door. During this part of their journey, the power of space has been neutralized (and therefore turned negative) by an inoffensive, yet overtly bland décor.

But once the owners open their own door, the power of the space turns overwhelmingly positive. The eyes are drawn to the fresh flowers always kept in the tall vase sitting on that lovely, uncluttered side table. The rectangular mirror behind the table reflects the painting on the opposite wall.

In this small entryway, the owners have created a tableau that helps them pause and soak in the moment. Their transitional zone, which highlights a touch of nature and a favorite painting, uses the power of space to their advantage. The minute they open the front door, they are welcomed inside. They feel good to be home.

THE PUBLIC HOME SPACE

After we open the front door of our house or apartment and step inside, we enter the second vastu classification of space connected to the home: the public space. Examples include the living room, dining room, den, and media room—all the areas where visitors and guests are likely to spend time. To understand the function of public spaces, let's think back to the old-fashioned parlor or sitting room, which was a staple in so many Victorian homes.

The parlor was designed to accommodate a wide range of social activities. There was room for a bridge table, where people played cards or board games. If the parlor had limited space, there were usually a collapsible bridge table and fold-up bridge chairs stored nearby. There was room for a piano or a phonograph, along with a storage compartment for a collection of popular ten-inch phonograph records. There was a carefully arranged seating area so that guests all felt welcomed—the introvert as well as the extrovert.

The well-organized parlor allowed for a diversity of personalities and social activities so that everyone in the room was able to relax. Nothing about the décor detracted from the function of the room: It was a welcoming space where families received and entertained guests.

Today, when I visit many of my clients, I notice that a mélange of furnishings and electronic products has blurred the ambience and obscured the function of their homes' public spaces. Many living rooms, in particular, are no longer designed to please the needs of the human body. Instead, they are organized to satisfy the quest for more and more electronic gadgets, more and more material possessions.

So many of us work hard to keep technology from controlling our lives, but we lose this battle when we let technology control the ambience in the public rooms of our homes. When electronics become the focus, they are impossible to avoid. We turn them on and they, in turn, turn us into passive creatures. We stop relating with one another and surrender our attention and time to the TV or computer.

These gadgets may connect users to the outside world, but they interfere with our ability to engage with the people closest to us—those who share our home. We cannot shut out the world; we need to be informed. But the strange, isolating nature of the office environment, where employees inhabit the same space but interact more often through their computer or on the telephone, is becoming the nature of our home environment as well. I have watched some of my clients communicate with another member of the family from room to room by cell phone or e-mail. How does this qualify as personal interaction?

Many people can't suppress the desire to acquire tantalizing new gadgets—but it is possible to learn to put them in their proper place, literally and figuratively. Again, think back to that old-fashioned parlor. The phonograph, the Victorian equivalent of today's media center, never took over a room. It was generally placed in a corner or along a side wall, where it could stay out of sight but still be accessible whenever anyone wanted to hear music.

The Wired Elephant Like most people, you probably have a TV in a public space in your home. Is it the dominating object, the first thing people notice when they enter the room? Is it instinctively turned on as if it were a light switch?

Consider this: Is it possible that you and your loved ones and guests spend more time watching TV than interacting with one another when you sit in this room?

For one week, keep a record of television time versus interaction time (and saying "pass the popcorn" doesn't count as interaction). You may discover that you need to reclaim the intended function of your living room and shift the location of the TV so that its screen no longer draws all eyes. This will help you shift priorities so that precious time is shared with one another—rather than getting swallowed up by the attention-grabbing TV.

Balancing Needs

A family living in a community not far from Manhattan has a busy daily schedule, juggling careers with the demands of home life. They were determined to strike a healthy balance between the convenience and pleasure of modern electronics and the need for time shared with one another. After they moved into their older Tudor-style house, they hired designer Kim Naylor from NICHE to help renovate it so that they could achieve their goal.

Once you step inside the renovated house, you enter its original center hall. The new décor is intentionally understated, with a judicious placement of objects that instinctively observe two of vastu's important principles, celebrating the beauty of nature and honoring the tastes and preferences of the family.

This central hall (see the images on pages 54 to 55) is so uncluttered that the eyes easily move from object to object. This absolute order creates a feeling of serenity and a soothing rhythm and flow. We feel the positive power of a space that welcomes people as they enter the house and gently reminds them to relax and leave distracting thoughts at the front door.

The center hall connects all the main areas of the home. A winding staircase provides access to the family bedrooms. A back corridor leads to the kitchen. Gracious French doors, one on either side of the hallway, open into two spacious public rooms.

In the center hall visitors encounter clues about the family who lives in this home: what they believe and what they love. Notice the shoes in front of the basket by the staircase. In many cultures, especially Eastern ones, people are expected to remove their shoes as they enter a house. This courtesy obviously connects to cleanliness: It prevents dirt being carried in from the external world where it would defile the interior of the house. But more importantly, the removal of shoes acknowledges the hallowed nature of the home. Just as the body is considered the temple of the soul, the home is considered the temple of the body.

The ritual act of removing shoes upon entering a house becomes a moment of conscious awareness. Those who participate in this ritual show respect for the home and, by extension, respect for the family and even themselves—because during this moment, they slow down and become mindful. This is the power of any ritual: It raises the level of an action that may normally be taken for granted and endows it with deeper meaning.

Another element of the décor in this center hall suggests a similar sacred ritual. A ceramic dish on the low credenza is the receptacle for cell phones, house and car keys, and loose change. Inside the home, the family members don't need these objects that they carry around with them in the exterior world.

The large mirror at the back of the credenza allows people who have just entered to catch a glimpse of what is not

LEFT: Tudor-home stairway.

RIGHT: Hallway credenza.

PAGES 56 TO 57:

LEFT: Tudor-home dining area.

RIGHT: Adjoining sitting area.

directly visible from the front door. It reflects the natural light from the windows that illuminates the plant placed inside each ornate niche. The sweet light creates a gentle flow that moves the eyes toward the upper floor.

This simple yet elegant center hall is a perfect introduction to the home and the people who live here. Even first-time visitors will notice the family's respect for Eastern cultures, made clear by the presence of the Asian statue on the credenza; their love of plants, which are showcased by natural light in the niches; and their appreciation of antiques.

The public room to the left of the center hall continues to reveal the priorities, interests, and tastes of the family. Notice the tapestries on the walls. Their dramatic expression of color, which captures our attention, celebrates the artistry of the wife, who created them.

In this particular public space, the family gathers to share meals at the dining room table. A spotlessly polished grand piano occupies another well-defined part of the room. Not far from the piano, a modern wool and silk rug demarcates an intimate seating area: a chair in a corner and a modern chaise.

Except for the bright pieces of fabric sewn into the tapestries, the surrounding décor is subdued—right down to the soothing wallpaper, created from silver paint brushed over thin sheets of cork.

The room's serene ambience is so appropriate for the functions attached to this

public space in the home. How easy to imagine taking the time to eat a delicious meal sitting under the soft light that bathes the dining room table. And who wouldn't enjoy relaxing quietly on the chaise to read a book or listen to someone play the piano?

The interior design in this room shows the ultimate truth of holism—the interconnectedness that binds together all creation. Every aspect of the décor comes together to create a cohesive whole, just as all the pieces of fabric come together to create the wall tapestries. Nothing is randomly placed. Nothing jars the eyes or bewilders the mind. Ambience and function exist in harmony, and the body, mind, and spirit feel good in this thoughtful space.

This multipurpose room illustrates one more truth about the appropriate décor for the public space in a home. The décor in the living room, dining room, media room—in all areas open to guests—should reveal, exclusively, our public face. These rooms should never broadcast the intimate details of our lives. Private objects belong in the bedrooms, which are normally off-limits to casual guests or strangers.

Lingering Warmth

The living room is on the other side of the center hall, directly across from the multipurpose dining and sitting room. The stately fireplace, with its asymmetrical display on the mantelpiece, appears framed by the dark wood encasing the doorway. The lighting above the fireplace casts soft shadows, which seem to form their own work of art on the wall. The distant fireplace and its carefully chosen artwork and lighting are so alluring that they draw the visitor in.

And once we're inside this public space, the asymmetrical sectional sofa and the matching pair of circular chairs encourage us to sit down, relax, and unwind. The thoughtful, uncluttered décor, dominated by its quiet colors, reinforces serenity and calm. We feel at ease in this living room, even if this is our first visit.

Symmetry or Asymmetry

Often when I am invited to sit in the living room of a client, I have an unfortunate visceral response. The sofa, chairs, and coffee table are frequently set apart at such an unaccommodating distance that everyone must lean forward to have a conversation. In addition, the layout of the furniture is unrelentingly symmetrical. The sofa is placed against the center of a wall. Chairs or a second sofa are directly across from it—forming two straight lines of furniture that face one another. The symmetry even extends to the placement of artwork on the walls.

My adverse reaction to the symmetrically-organized living room is not abnormal. This arrangement ignores the comfort preferences of the human body—our innate tendency to position our body asymmetrically. Everything in a symmetrical room tells us sit

LEFT: View into the living room.

ABOVE: Living room tapestry.

RIGHT: A touch of symmetry.

PAGE 62: The calming power of asymmetry.

up straight, don't cross the legs, don't lean left or right. We turn formal and stiff, and even, at times, unsociable and eager to leave.

But in this transformed Tudor home, the ambience of the handsome living room matches function. Its décor, while minimal and understated, expresses welcome and makes the body feel at ease.

Notice, though, that the room is not devoid of symmetry. For example, the TV screen is centered on the side wall, and the two circular chairs are positioned symmetrically. This placement is judicious and makes sense. This same room functions as the family's media center, which is integrated discreetly into the décor. We don't notice the flat screen TV when we first enter the room, and we don't notice the audio system, which is hidden behind the frosted glass doors of the low console that extends across much of the sidewall.

The choice of the two round chairs is accommodating. When the family and its guests want to watch TV or a DVD, everyone can see the screen. The people sitting in the chairs simply swivel them around. Only then is the TV the center of attention.

Healthy By Design

In addition to the fireplace, the Eastern shoji screens, which cover the Tudor-pane windows, add special warmth to the ambience. The screens reinforce all three principles of vastu. When they are opened in the morning,

rejuvenating sunlight flows into the room. As the sun's heat intensifies during the course of the day, they can be adjusted to block out the unhealthy rays. The organic screens, with their natural blond wood, also honor nature. Finally, their Eastern design celebrates the interests and preferences of the family who lives here.

Take a Lingering Look

When you start to design and organize your own living or dining room, remember that your choice of décor, modern or Victorian or eclectic, has no bearing on the creation of an appealing public space. Just look at the following lovely rooms. The first three images show public spaces in a Hawaiian home designed by Sarah Susanka, the successful architect and author. The final image shows a stylish dining room in a loft designed by Doug Atherley, the founder of London-based Kinari Design.

Each of these successful rooms created by a talented professional exhibits a vision that satisfies the particular needs of the client. But both visions match ambience to function and both rooms respect the preferences of the human body.

THE PRIVATE SPACE

It amazes me how many of my clients' bedrooms, kitchens, and bathrooms exhibit an ambience that is painfully out of alignment with the function of the room. The bedroom is neither tranquil nor personal. The kitchen is overwhelmed by an accumulation of stuff that has nothing to do with eating. The bathroom is cold and lacks a defining décor.

Before considering each of these rooms, which are the private spaces in the home, let's go back many years, to a time when the home was more than the backdrop for memories. The home was woven into the design of the memory itself. The oak desk in the bedroom hid a youngster's private diaries that held precious secrets. The mirror in the bathroom was where the young adults shaved or put on lipstick for the very first time. The wood table in the kitchen was where they sat at dinner time and told the family about their triumphs, disappointments, and sorrows. The home was the center of family life. It existed as a cherished place that was all about us. It was a special gathering place—where the family came together to reenact the rituals that became the fixed memories they carried through their lives.

Think about the arrangement of the décor in your living room. Does it add up to an inviting ambience that supports the function of this important public space in your home? Do your guests sit comfortably in your chairs and sofa? Do they relax and linger? In other words, is the room livable? Or have you inadvertently created a dead room?

LEFT, RIGHT, AND PAGE 66:
At home in Hawaii.

ABOVE: Loft dining room.

How therapeutic it would be for us if we could reconnect to the rituals that were once so tightly bound to these three special environments. These rituals enhance our well-being and have the same effect on us as the chorus in a song. By repeating these rituals again and again, they penetrate our heart and soul.

Today, however, the home has run into stiff competition as the family gathering place, and it is less often the locus of important memories. These days, celebrations for family milestones rarely occur in dens or living rooms. Most such events are celebrated outside the home in restaurants or other impersonal public environments. The rituals that once bound the family together have begun to unravel. This is most apparent in the three private spaces that exist in every home: the bedroom, kitchen, and bathroom.

From the vastu perspective, these three spaces connect to the critical daily rituals that define the cycle of life. The bedroom connects to the ritual of creation; the kitchen connects to the ritual of preservation; the bathroom connects to the ritual of destruction. Such associations may seem like hyperbole, but let's examine the correlations. You may be surprised to see how far we have distanced ourselves from understanding the significance behind these three intimate spaces that exist in every home.

The Power of the Bedroom

It's easy to understand why an adult bedroom ties to the ritual of creation, but you may wonder why a child's bedroom reflects the same ritual. Think about children—and how creativity breathes life into their new ideas and beliefs and into their most tender and fragile aspirations and dreams.

When children play or relax in the bedroom, they should feel free to be in their own private space. The décor should be theirs, encouraging them to open up completely, to feel unconstrained—not physically, necessarily, but emotionally and mentally. The power of this space, the bedroom, should be so positive, so reinforcing, that it nurtures the instinctive creativity within every child.

By thinking about this personal space from the vastu perspective, we see the value of dedicating every bedroom to the act of creativity. And since all creation is divine, every bedroom in the home is not just a private space, it is a sacred place that honors our divinity.

Many of us probably never connect such profound meanings to the bedroom, but think about this: Do you feel comfortable when visitors come into your bedroom—or does your closed bedroom door signal the limits to your hospitality? Many of us only invite family members or dear friends and lovers into this intimate space. Instinctively, we treat this room differently than we treat any other in our home. And when most of us are obliged to enter the bedroom of a stranger or casual acquaintance—say, to use an attached bathroom or leave a coat on the bed during a party—we feel uncomfortable, like a trespasser violating someone's intimate space.

This is the appropriate reaction to a well-designed bedroom; it indicates the successful match between ambience and function. The bedroom that connects intimately to the individual or individuals who sleep in it expresses the private face—as opposed to the public face, which is on display in the public spaces of a home.

The intimate décor in a bedroom can make its occupant feel secure. When we slip into bed and prepare to drift off to sleep, the bedroom feels like a protective outer layer that safeguards the body and soul. Connecting deeply to an intimate décor helps us relax and fall asleep. And a healthy sleep does more than enhance well-being; it boosts the power of creativity. Recent research has proven that the ability to learn improves after a good night's rest.

Restful Havens

The two bedrooms shown in the following pictures are vastu-perfect. The first is in the Santa Fe home of Paula Baker-Laporte and Robert Laporte, the founders of EcoNest. It is ideally designed for sleeping—no physical clutter, which could stir up the mind, exists in it anywhere.

The ochre hue of the walls, which are coated with a plaster wash of clay and straw,

is calming. So is the intentional symmetry created by the placement of the matching tables and lamps on either side of the bed. The symmetry draws the eyes to the bed's surface, and its shape helps still the mind. This is true with all square-based shapes, as you will learn in Chapter Five, "Defining Details."

The placement of the bed in the southwest of the room, however, is asymmetrical; so, in fact, the overall design of the bedroom conforms to the vastu-preference for asymmetrical layouts. By opening up the north and east, this placement prevents the small room from feeling claustrophobic. The undecorated walls also contribute to the feeling of openness. We don't think of them as incomplete or barren. Simplicity is on display, and this simplicity, which wraps completely around us, is easy on the eye.

The room's simplicity reinforces the function of the bedroom and of sleep. The empty walls remind guests to empty their minds when they slip into bed. By emptying the mind of thoughts that can interfere with sleep, we are more apt to wake up refreshed.

The open northeastern corner of this room is calming for an additional reason: In vastu, the northeast is considered the gateway to the gods. As I noted earlier, this direction, which yogis used to face when they did their yogic postures and meditation, receives the gentle light of the morning sun. This early morning light is emotionally, mentally, and physically healing.

ABOVE: Santa Fe bedroom.

RIGHT: Mindful display of photos.

To draw attention to this corner of the room, Paula and Robert have arranged a personally meaningful display of photos on a simple rectangular table. When the shade is raised in the morning, the sun flows into the room and bathes the table and its display in light. Even when the shade is drawn, the light on the wall illuminates the images.

I encourage my clients to place a similarly meaningful display, which I call a zone of tranquility, in the northeastern quadrant of every room, especially in the bedroom, where it can inspire positive thoughts and feelings when they wake up in the morning and face this direction. Clearly, the display in the picture on this page is an expression of love that warms the heart, even the hearts of the guests who spend the night here. Every photo on the table celebrates this family and the people they love.

The second bedroom, also a guest bedroom, is in the western New York home of an artist and her husband, an optometrist. The architect Mary Golden, who founded Gaiatecture Design Studio, specializes in straw bale homes and did the pleasing trowel-worked sculpting of the plaster (which is made of clay, sand, chopped straw, and water) around the windows. She and the artist then applied the finishing coat of golden-hued clay on two of the thick straw bale walls. Their lovely sparkle comes from flecks of mica, a natural component of the clay.

This guest bedroom is small, but Mary

NEAR RIGHT: Western New York bedroom.

FAR RIGHT: Meaningful details.

and the artist organized the furniture so that it feels intimate, not cramped. The dominant colors, soft pastels and earth tones, and the carefully selected organic materials create a quiet ambience, which, once again, matches the function of the room. It is clearly designed for sleeping.

And yes, there are objects galore, but they celebrate the world of nature and the personal lives and interests of this particular couple in rural New York. Their choices, from the husband's old harness boots on the floor to the pitchfork with some of the artist's jewelry hung between the prongs and the felt pouch she made for the plant on the windowsill, bring order to this room. Harmony and balance prevail, and guests who stay here are keenly aware of the attention to detail; it reminds them that this care extends to them. They are welcome in this home.

Dream Rooms

Study three more bedrooms, in the following pages, to see how designers and their clients have created a restful and personal ambience. The first bedroom is in another vastu home designed by EcoNest for a young couple. The grounding colors of the clay-washed walls, muted lighting, and lovely simplicity are reassuring; so is the personalized shrine set into the wall opposite the bed. The Buddhist deity and flowers greet the young couple when they awaken and watch over them while they sleep.

The second bedroom is in a home designed by the thoughtful and detail-oriented architect Sarah Susanka to celebrate the owners' appreciation of art. The placement of the bed enables the couple to wake up each morning to see an example of the modern artwork that they love so much. The painting's colors are vibrant, but the bedroom's otherwise quiet décor, accentuated by the warm wood floor and the soft lighting, allows an easy calm to assert itself.

The third bedroom was created by the visually eloquent designer Clodagh for one of her clients. It shows the power of the asymmetry achieved by placing the bed in the corner. The room feels delightfully spacious, while the pillows on the bed and the positioning of the Buddha and the candle cast an aura of serenity through the private space.

Just as each public space described in this chapter expresses its own distinct décor, each of these bedrooms reveals its own set of preferences that reflect the special interests of the homeowners. And the designers who created these rooms understand the nature of the ambience that belongs in this private space—each bedroom is intimate and designed for deep sleep.

LEFT: Sacred display.

RIGHT: Bedroom designed by EcoNest.

ABOVE: Bedroom designed by Sarah Susanka.

RIGHT: Bedroom designed by Clodagh.

The Power of the Kitchen

In the past, the kitchen was generally off-limits to most guests in the home. It was considered a private space where mothers prepared the day's meals and the entire family sat down to eat supper together. The old-fashioned kitchen faithfully honored the rituals that celebrated this act of preservation. Many families said grace together before they started to eat; they ate home-cooked meals slowly and with few distractions, because the ambience in this private space was exclusively about food and nourishment.

But today's kitchen is a lot different. For starters, this room is frequently the most popular and populated space in the home. Not only are guests welcome there, everything else ends up there, too. No other part of the house or apartment gets as cluttered as the modern-day kitchen. Objects are piled on every surface, and these surfaces are usually out in the open.

The "look" of this important room no longer focuses exclusively on food and nourishment. This change, in turn, has derailed the rituals that used to accompany mealtime, and their absence has interfered with our ability to enjoy cooking. And yes, cooking should be fun. Cooking provides a reliable way to relax and unwind.

But today, many of us think of cooking as a chore. We feel so chronically rushed that we can't let ourselves get into the rituals attached to the art of cooking. In a practical sense, kitchen clutter interferes with the ability to cook or even enjoy a meal. Instead of paying attention to the food on our plate, we are distracted by the un-kitchen-related material surrounding us.

Kitchen clutter creates a negative décor that may help explain why so many of us eat standing up these days. Reminders of work to be done or other responsibilities vie for our attention and time. The mess encourages us to eat on the go so we can get on to something else. Or it may be so visually unappealing, literally unappetizing, that it encourages us to get out of the room. The invasion of objects creates a negative décor, which unleashes the power of negative space and sets in motion the act of avoidance.

When preparing a meal, our actions, from the chopping of fruits and vegetables to the sautéing of sizzling ingredients, should

---

Make a list of all the things in your kitchen that have nothing to do with food and food preparation. Remove as many of these objects as you can. How does the ambience change? Now add details that celebrate the importance and beauty of food, such as a window-box herb garden, a basket of fresh fruit or vegetables, or a rope of garlic. How do these food-related details affect the ambience? Can you feel the difference?

delight all the senses. As we sit down to share a meal, the table setting and food presentation should encourage us to enjoy the rituals associated with eating, to savor the variety of tastes and the shared time with our dining companions. This is an important time: We are nourishing our body and taking care to keep it healthy so the body can take care of our soul.

The ambience in the two kitchens shown on these pages supports the room's function. Both rooms, which are in Santa Fe and were created by Paula Baker-Laporte and Robert Laporte of EcoNest, are free of unnecessary clutter. Every element in their design reinforces the pleasures associated with food and the act of nourishing the body.

The kitchen on pages 79 to 81 belongs to Paula and Robert. This space is a model of efficiency, with cupboards and wall units conveniently positioned for easy access to all their cooking needs. The clutter-free counters provide ample room to prepare an array of dishes. Many of their ingredients come from Paula's organic vegetable garden (page 83), which is just outside the kitchen door. This kitchen would easily please any cook who doesn't want distractions—other than the spectacular mountain view—to get in the way of the preparation of the meal.

The second kitchen, in a vastu home designed by EcoNest for a young couple and their child, reveals a similar absence of clutter. The room, on page 82, evokes calm, serenity

even, through the family's choice of personalized details. Buddha reigns over a collection of teapots and a row of ceramic bowls. The prominent placement of a sacred object in the kitchen reinforces the significance that this young couple, who are yoga teachers, attach to their kitchen and home.

The Power of the Bathroom

So many of us are willing to spend money periodically at an expensive spa so that we can pamper ourselves and our body. Shouldn't we be pampering ourselves daily in our own home? Most of us rarely do this. Instead, we tend to speed through the moments that are spent in this private room—a clear sign that we are probably just as guilty of taking shortcuts with our overall well-being.

The power of this private space ought to be used to healthy advantage. The bathroom should be considered sacred. It is a retreat where we go to care for the temple of the soul, where we rid our body of its daily accumulation of pollutants and toxins.

So how is it possible to create an ambience that helps develop healthy rituals that are tied to the act of destruction and yet clearly benefit the body? Start by reviewing a list of priorities. Far too often, the designer in us dismisses the appearance of the bathroom as being of small importance. We tell ourselves that we'll deal with it sometime in the future. But the

ABOVE: Paula's organic garden.

future can never become the present, and truth be told, many people don't even *think* about the importance of this special space.

Yes, it is true that most of us work hard to keep the bathroom clean. We apply anti-bacterial and antifungal agents to keep the floor, tiles, and fixtures mold- and germ-free. Many of us also attempt to dilute the bathroom's medicinal sheen with a set of towels and a shower curtain that add color to the room. But this still leaves a negative space that feels cool (as in cold) and clinical (as in a surgical room in the hospital). Just as no one wants to linger in a hospital, no one wants to linger in an uninviting bathroom. No wonder so many of us fail to cultivate the pleasurable and meaningful rituals that honor the physical body and make us feel good about ourselves.

The antidote to the bathroom's cold décor is warmth, the calming and inspiring warmth that comes from the sun, from nature, from a personalized space that connects to us viscerally and visually. By creating the right décor in a bathroom, we create a space that encourages us to take our time in this important space.

Let's look at four bathrooms, each different in décor and design. Each reflects design choices dictated by the physical lay-out of the space or the individual needs and preferences of the people who use these rooms. But all four create an ambience that supports the function of this sacred room.

FAR LEFT: Western New York bathroom.

NEAR LEFT: Straw bale bathroom in California.

NEAR RIGHT: New York City loft bathroom.

FAR RIGHT: Loft bathroom details.

The first bathroom, in the home of the artist and her husband in western New York, provides natural light to accompany the view of the trees outside the window. That view is reflected in the mirror, along with the artist's felt artwork, which hangs on the wall. The couple's appreciation of nature and recycled treasures is expressed through the careful placement of the seashells peeking out of the basket, the painted rock on the floor, the doily ensconced in the old rectangular mirror, and the reclaimed claw-foot bathtub.

The sun is the inspiration behind the second bathroom, which is in a California straw bale home designed by Kelly Lerner of One World Design and Peter Gang of Common Sense Design. Sunlight flows into this private space from the skylight and the window, enhancing the soft palette of the ceiling, with its reed matting, and the clay-washed walls. It warms the porcelain tub and anyone reclining inside it.

This positive space would make any one of us feel a bit lazy if we were to enter the room. The bathroom décor says stay awhile. Empty your mind while you soak in all this appealing warmth.

The third bathroom, which is designed by thread collective, an architectural firm in New York City, has no windows or sky-lights. It provides no view of the sun or any part of the natural world outside the home. This windowless bathroom is deep inside

an upper-floor loft building, but it evokes warmth, nonetheless. It draws upon the power of serenity to establish an emotionally warm, sacred space.

The bathroom is adjacent to the master bedroom, and it is entered through a dressing room, where the sheen of the dark wood shelving and the closets reflects the glow of the bathroom lighting. The dark dressing room, which is the height of orderliness, doubles as a laundry room. The washing machine is concealed when not in use.

Dark wood frames the bathroom, which becomes our focal point. Its quiet aura draws our eyes into the distant space.

Every aspect of the décor and design of this bathroom reinforces the feeling of tranquillity. The three niches on the sidewall contain carefully chosen objects that work together to create an appealing vision of serenity. The two identical square sinks and rectangular mirrors are also symbolically and visually potent. Showers often encourage a hurried dousing, but this one is transformed into a space that invites lingering: The square-based enclosure, with its organic walls and floor, and the beckoning dark wood bench offer a place to sit down and spend time.

The last bathroom, designed by Bruno Bondanelli, the Italian architect who founded Los Angeles-based Designx, incorporates the eclectic tastes of the owners of this Hollywood home.

LEFT: Dressing room and bathroom.

The enormous size of the tub is ideal for luxuriating in foot-deep soapy water, but we are most likely to notice the unexpected comfy chair and bench with its wine-color pillows before focusing on the tub. Whimsy is foremost in this bathroom, where the spacious room also invites the sunlight. Its warmth reaches into the space from two different directions, with its intensity controlled by the Venetian blinds and their bow-tied sashes. Nature is honored in the display of plants in the corner—the soothing green of the leaves becomes a meditatively pleasing source of inspiration to the bather reclining in the tub.

This fourth bathroom sums up the point of these first two chapters. Match ambience to function and you lay the proper foundation for taking advantage of the positive power inherent in every space. Now you are ready to learn about the design components required to create the appropriate ambience. The first important matter of space that we will examine is light—not merely light, but the dance between light and shadow.

LEFT: New York City loft shower cubicle.

RIGHT: Hollywood bathroom.

Everything that exists has an opposing force—and these forces, or dualities, enrich our appreciation of our world. After all, how can we enjoy the sunlight unless we experience the darkness of night?

CHAPTER THREE:
Light and Shadow—Welcome Their Dance

During the earliest years of life, when children begin to take note of their surroundings, they slowly become aware of the dualities that exist around them. The presence of light and dark, hot and cold, wet and dry—the list of oppositional forces goes on and on. All these dualities create the rhythms that flow in the universe and that, in turn, protect the order and balance so necessary for the earth's survival.

Such dualities shape our earliest perceptions of the physical world. We notice, in particular, the movement of light and dark that governs the passage of time, but we are unable to understand that concept in our early years. Lullabies sung in lowered voices marked the evening, the beginning of the darkness, when we were apt to be cradled and given a bottle of milk in preparation for sleep. At daybreak, another set of sounds and activities stirred us from slumber. We heard the morning calls of early-rising birds or the trill of the alarm clock signaling the start of a new workday for Mother and Father; we feel the warmth of the sun's early rays that flowed into our nursery and reached inside the crib.

Dualities are also instructive. They help establish the important moral and ethical boundaries that mold behavior and our healthy interaction with family and community. As time passes, we are introduced, one by one, to the abstract dualities that bring order and harmony to the world. We come to understand such terms as right and wrong, good and bad, yes and no—and because pleasure is generally preferred over pain and acceptance is better than rejection, we modify and model our behavior to fit in and find our way. These linked pairs of opposites serve as both teacher and ongoing source of inspiration.

The Power of Light

Light and dark. Morning and night. Sunrise and sunset. These are just a few of the ways to define the dominant duality that governs life in this world. As I pointed out in Chapter One, "Design to Please the Human Body," the role of light and dark and its influence on us and all other living creatures is unrivaled in the universal scheme of things. No wonder the concepts of light and dark can serve as such powerful metaphors. When light dispels darkness, awareness overcomes ignorance. Those who "see the light" are granted the ability to distinguish fact from fiction.

Sunlight warms us when it removes the chill of darkness. It comforts us as it illuminates what had become invisible during the night. Sunlight even brightens our mood. Medical research has documented that it stimulates the production of serotonin, a mood-lifting chemical, in the pineal gland at the base of the brain. Perhaps our emotional response to sunlight explains why so many people find the transition from light to dark or dark to light so deeply compelling.

Most of us also appreciate the changing quality of light. Remember the last time you sat before a campfire or a crackling fire in a fireplace? Live flames, as they shoot up and retreat with bursts of radiant color, can be mesmerizing. Often we sit in silence just watching until the fire dies down or the heat forces us to move away.

Just as a quiet walk in the woods can be calming, so can the flickering colors of the fire. The flames inspire a state of quiescence. Like nature, this dance of light has the ability to connect us to deeper thoughts and spark inspirations that put us in spirit. We can hear our inner voice.

We thrive on the interplay between the dualities of light and dark, yet few of us consciously plan for its presence inside the home. Few of us think about the dance between light and shadow at all, or know how to think about lighting, in general, so its power can be used to our advantage.

As a result, when dealing with light and lighting in the home, most of us end up confusing our priorities. If we are considering window treatments for windows, we tend to focus on the look of a particular blind or shade or drape. Similarly, when thinking about adding artificial light to a room, we dwell on the specific lighting fixture, not the quality of the illumination.

To address this critical matter of space, we must first understand that all lighting, natural or artificial, should support

ARTIFICIAL LIGHTING
USUALLY SERVES ONE OF THREE FUNCTIONS. LET'S LEARN BRIEFLY ABOUT EACH OF THEM:

Ambient Lighting

Ambient lighting, which very often shines down from the ceiling, spreads light evenly around a room. It is called ambient because it surrounds the room's occupants and has the power to manipulate their mood. When adding ambient lighting into any area of the home, think carefully about the quality of the light—its brightness and color. Make certain that your choice reinforces the function of the room and contributes positively to the ambience.

Task Lighting

The name says it all. Task lighting provides strong, localized light in a specific area of a room so you can see what you are doing. With task lighting, you must always choose the proper intensity. A dim reading lamp defeats its purpose. Be sure that the fixture allows you to use the right power of bulb for the task at hand. Again, function matters.

Accent Lighting

Accent lighting draws attention to a specific object or display inside your home. It may highlight an architectural detail or purposely cast a wider swath of light onto a wall to create the dance of light and shadow. Used creatively, accent lighting can become a work of art itself.

the ambience and function of the room. There is no exception to this rule. Start by considering the intended function of the actual lighting. Why do you want to add light to the space? Imagine sitting at a dining room table that has the bright lighting of a fast-food joint. The lighting there matches the function of that place: its brightness is energizing and encourages people to eat quickly and leave. In a dining room at home, the goal is for everyone to relax and enjoy the meal, the company, and the shared time.

Seeing is believing. So let's examine the lighting in two different environments: a dining room created by the designer Clodagh and a typical fast-food restaurant.

Do you see how the lighting affects the ambience and supports the function of each space? Notice, in particular, the lovely effect of the dance of light and shadow in the dining room: We can feel the power of the lighting, beyond just seeing it with our eyes. These environments show not only the power of light to shape the ambience in a space, but the ultimate power of our own choices for the lighting in every area of the home.

LEFT: Typical fast-food lighting.

RIGHT: Gracious dining.

The Power of Color

The power of color to affect emotions mirrors the power of light. This makes sense because the white light of the sun contains the seven colors in the visible spectrum: red, orange, yellow, green, blue, indigo, and violet. These are the colors of every rainbow that shimmers in the sky.

When gazing into a rainbow, our eyes interact with each color's distinct pattern of energy or wavelength, which is released by the sun. These wavelengths create their own vibrations, and the unique nature of each vibration stimulates the retina, determining the specific color perceived.

Red has the longest wavelength and is always at the top of the rainbow (unless you are doubly lucky and see a double rainbow, which includes a fainter, second arc, where the colors in the visible spectrum appear in the opposite order).

After red come orange, yellow, green, blue, indigo, and finally violet, which has the shortest wavelength. Violet is the most difficult arc to see in the rainbow and always appears closest to the ground.

The rainbow illustrates another example of the law of nature that is central to Vedic philosophy. Even in its seemingly miraculous display, there is nothing random in a rainbow's creation, neither in the order of its display of color nor in the properties attached to each color. And there is nothing random in the effect that each color or white light, the sum total of the seven colors, has on life forms.

CHOOSING THE RIGHT COLOR

Most of us struggle to determine the appropriate lighting, and our anxiety intensifies when we are faced with choosing the appropriate color or colors for a room. Most of us usually pick the color of the clothes we wear and adamantly defend our color preferences. But conviction withers when it comes to colors for a home. We agonize over the endless possibilities, timidity and confusion preventing us from making a firm decision.

But if every color quest is based on the principle that ambience must support function, decisions can be made with confidence. Color has a critical impact on the ambience of a room. Color can energize, calm, create warmth or coolness (as in

aloofness). In fact, each color in the visible spectrum triggers predictable emotional reactions common to all of us. The following chart describes the emotional properties of each of the seven colors and white.

As we all know from trips to the paint store, the colors in the visible spectrum can be combined in innumerable ways. At the store, we end up staring at a wall filled with color chips. How is it possible to determine the emotional properties of all these colors? After all, aqua feels different from navy blue; lime yellow feels different from deep gold; tan feels different from dark brown.

Let's consider two shades of the color red. The bright red of the stop sign at left is quite close to the pure red of the visible spectrum. Unless they're distracted, drivers can always see a stop sign at the side of the road, just as the bull in the ring always sees the waving red cape. Drivers heed its message. They stop. The red of the stop sign is true to the properties described in the following chart; this red on the walls of a room would make a commanding, bold statement. It would energize the ambience.

Now let's examine the darker red on the wall in the upper right photo. This hue is close to burgundy, and its emotional properties reflect its mix of red with darker colors on the spectrum, such as blue, indigo, and violet. The color feels calm and makes the surface of the wall look velvety soft. This red is appropriate

for the ambience of the bedroom. It is soothing and serene.

So, with color, remember that your final choice should observe the rule that ambience supports function. When you narrow down the selection for a room in your home, put all choices to this final test: Purchase a small can of each color and apply each to a part of the same area in the room that you intend to paint. Over the next couple of days, examine each color under different lighting conditions. Let more than your eyes be the judge. Feel your reaction to each color. Does it make you feel like relaxing and slowing down or does it make you feel more animated? Does it make you feel warm or cool? And always, always ask whether the color on the wall enhances the ambience and supports the function of the room. The appropriate color requires the answer yes!

FEEL THE POWER

Once again, the best way to understand the power of color is to look at environments created by great designers and architects. Since color and light are related and work together, notice how the two of them contribute substantially to the creation of the appropriate ambience.

The hallway and bedroom at right are in a straw bale home created by Kelly Lerner of One World Design and Peter Gang of Creative Design. The space is organic, yet dreamy, nearly ethereal, in appearance. The sand-hued, clay-washed walls, with scrollwork detail above the arch, perfectly frame the bedroom with its indigo clay-washed walls and décor dominated by the purity of white.

The sheer curtains that cover the bank of doors leading to a terrace soften the day's bright sun. The resulting gentle light enters the interior of this private space contributing to the stillness and quiet. Although the sunlight is moderated, we sense the quality of the day unfolding behind the thin panels of white fabric.

The reading area, on page 108, which is on the ground floor of the same straw bale home, is pleasing and inviting. The light streaming into the room adds to the warm ambience created by the earth plaster on the walls and the reed matting on the ceiling. The simple furniture looks comfy. This is a good place to sit and read or just stare outside for hours.

The room shown on page 109 is in another straw bale home designed by Kelly Lerner. Notice how the light and shadows dance across the earthen walls, floor, and all other surfaces.

The moody lighting in the bedroom creates an ambience that appeals to the eyes and wins over the soul. The bedroom encourages its occupants to stretch out on the handsome bed and admire the view outside in the daytime or close their eyes for a restful sleep at night.

The rooms on pages 110 to 117 are in a straw bale home designed by Susie Harrington and Kalen Jones, who founded With Gaia Design. Imagine the exterior world, which is dominated by southeastern Utah's rugged, sun-drenched vistas. How wonderful it must feel to step inside this home and remove our shoes. The interior, with its strong colors, provides a refreshing escape from the parched colors outside the door.

The ambient lighting is also intentionally gentle inside the home, yet in every room the dance of light and shadow still highlights, and at times mirrors, the architectural details that have been incorporated into the design. Notice, in particular, how the diagonal archway that leads into the kitchen and dining area mirrors the angle of the natural light flowing through the windows into the living room and the front entryway.

The alcove on page 118 is in a home created by Sarah Susanka. The large windows

LEFT: Bedroom in a straw bale home.

THESE PAGES AND PAGES 108 TO 109:

Various straw bale homes.

Notice the window treatments: the natural fiber, woven shades that moderate the daylight. Just as walkers in a leafy grove catch glimpses of natural light as it filters through an arcade of branches, the people in this room see the diffuse daylight even when the shade is drawn.

The wood floor, with its subtly changing tones, accentuates the movement of light; so does the door, which is literally a work of art— a series of acrylic transparencies sandwiched together form the door. Created by the artist Tony Conway, this door, which is so visually and viscerally pleasing, is an inspired touch, with its choice of colors associated with wisdom and enlightenment. The square center even reinforces this association. The illuminated square niches, embedded in the upper part of the wall, further enhance the calm that circulates through this room.

The feelings inspired by this room continue after sunset. At night, the gentle light from the square niches is augmented by the dimly lit recessed ceiling lighting and the flickering flames of candles. The emotional warmth of this environment remains constant and true.

The room's ambience consistently supports the function of the dining room. It also supports all the rituals we should celebrate at mealtime. Clodagh's careful design clearly shows how the positive use of the powers of color, light, and space can create an idyllic room worthy of inclusion in that special place we call home.

invite the play of light and shadow into the room, and the detailing on the window frame recalls a Buddhist mandala. The grounded, square shape adds to the feeling of calm in this intimate space.

Every design choice that Clodagh has made in the dining room on page 119 expresses the emotional role light can play in a home.

FAR LEFT AND NEAR LEFT: Entryway in
Utah home by Gaia Design.

LEFT AND RIGHT: Utah kitchen.

LEFT: "Saloon" pantry doors.

RIGHT: View into kitchen.

LEFT: Organic beauty.

RIGHT: Utah living room.

PAGES 118 TO 119:

RIGHT: Dining room designed by Clodogh.

LEFT: Alcove designed by Susanka.

Celebrate your
interconnection with
nature and bring it into
your home. Let its
power and quiet beauty
inspire you.

CHAPTER FOUR:
The Healing Touch of Nature—Aim for Organic

A weeping willow with spring leaves that dip down to new grass. The sweet, earthy odor of moist soil after a summer rainfall. The crunch of autumn leaves and the fragrance of pinecones that accompany a hike in the woods. The joy of winter daybreak, when dreamy, soft colors break through a cold night's darkness. Such special moments make us keenly aware of humanity's bond with nature. Instinctively, we know that we are kindred spirits.

The Vedic scholars who created vastu were so committed to the theory of holism that it assumed a spiritual dimension for them. Historically, the practice of vastu showed a profound and unlimited reverence for all creation. When timber was required to construct a building, the trees were sanctified before being removed from the forest. Creatures that inhabited each tree were entreated to leave so that no harm would befall them. The ax was washed and blessed before it was used. And once the tree fell, it was sheltered for months so that its wounds could heal. Only then would it be used for construction. Other life forms, and even stones that were disturbed during the process of building a structure, received this level of respect, reverence, and careful handling.

Vastu is so environmentally conscious that it is conceivably the oldest holistic architectural and design science. It is surely the ancient precursor to today's science of ecology and the green building movement. The Vedic scholars, who understood that holism creates the order and harmony that exist in the world, believed that when we cut ourselves off from nature, we disturb our symbiotic relationship with the external environment in subtle yet injurious ways.

For us to remain healthy, these scholars believed that we must welcome nature into the home. And their interpretation of nature encompassed every created aspect of the universe, from the flora and fauna to the rocks and metals hidden inside the earth. Their reverence for the environment, heightened by their commitment to holism, became the second principle of vastu. These scholars understood that nature's presence brought joy and health to the human spirit.

Bringing Nature into the Home

In this modern world, many of us need to shift the way we think about nature and how we use it inside our house or apartment. Too often nature is considered a decorative accessory—brought inside to make visual statements by adding some color or texture. This limited view of the value of nature reduces its extraordinary power to enhance our lives.

Consider how it feels to take a quiet walk along the beach or a stroll in a park. You can be grieving or frustrated by a seemingly intractable problem, and suddenly, and often unexpectedly, your spirits lift or the missing solution reveals itself. The Vedic scholars were right: Nature is a remarkable source of inspiration. It belongs in an authentic home so that this special space, the one true sanctuary, can inspire us.

Yet many people, while not consciously shunning nature, too easily choose synthetic products for the home. And unlike the positive power of nature, the power attached to synthetic products is negative: They can even be harmful to our health.

I frequently see the consequences of synthetics when I visit clients' homes and am ushered into rooms that are almost entirely artificial. The drapes, the carpeting, and the furniture upholstery are all man-made polyester fabrics; the few natural products, plants or glass objects (glass is made from sand), are swallowed up by the overwhelmingly synthetic décor.

The artificiality of these personal environments spreads into the ambience, and each of these rooms ends up exemplifying the décor of disconnect. By failing to honor holism, failing to reflect the power of nature, these rooms do not celebrate an interconnection with and interdependence on all that exists. When I sit in these rooms, I feel stuck inside an unreal space. Ultimately, the absence of nature in a home cuts us off from an essential part of ourselves.

Pollutants: Unwanted Guests

Always think carefully, very carefully, about the composition of the objects that you plan to introduce into your personal surroundings. Remember that synthetic materials, which have the capacity to harm the outdoor environment, also have the capacity to harm us inside the home.

Let's look at the results of important studies that have evaluated the quality of the air that circulates in buildings, in general, and in houses, in particular. The U.S. Environmental Protection Agency's booklet *The Inside Story: A Guide to Indoor Air Quality* (1995) reports that the air inside the home can be many times more polluted than the air outside. This holds true for homes in rural areas and in heavily industrialized urban centers. This is one alarming instance where location, location, location doesn't make a difference.

Many of the harmful chemicals in personal surroundings are odorless and invisible. They quietly injure without warning—until, perhaps, it is too late. Among these dangerous pollutants are carcinogens, neurotoxins (which can damage nerve tissue), or substances disruptive to the normal functions attached to cell growth and the body's elaborate endocrine system, which controls the glands and hormones. Indoor pollutants have also been linked to the rise in asthma and other respiratory ailments, skin disorders, and even an increase in learning disabilities.

Indeed, babies and children are particularly vulnerable to the presence of chemicals in the home because their young immune systems are not yet fully developed. The tiniest members of our families also live closer to the ground: They crawl and love to put their little fingers, along with traces of whatever they have touched, into their mouths. But all of us, whatever our age or size, can suffer adversely from the presence of these dangerous substances.

THE UNWANTED LIST

Thousands of man-made products contain chemicals considered hazardous to our health. Let's look at one group of chemicals called volatile organic compounds (VOCs). In this case, the word organic refers to the presence of carbon, which appears in nearly every biological compound. The word volatile refers to the fact that VOCs, which exist in liquid or solid form, emit vapors into the air.

People worry about VOCs seeping into the outdoor air and the groundwater, where they can do considerable harm. But many of us unwittingly introduce them into our own homes. In a study of six American communities undertaken in the late 1980s and described in "The Inside Story", the EPA discovered that the level of VOCs was ten times higher indoors than out of doors, "even in locations with significant outdoor air pollution sources, such as petrochemical plants."

Formaldehyde, often found in the glue used to install wall-to-wall carpets, is a dangerous VOC. It may be underfoot right now as you read this book. Or it may be under a nearby area rug; it can be an ingredient in the varnish that gives a wood floor its lovely sheen. Formaldehyde can be found in some particle board and pressed wood products such as plywood, commonly used for furniture in the home.

Or maybe the formaldehyde is in the paint you used to add a splash of new color to the walls in the dining room. Yes, when you rolled on the paint, you probably followed the instructions on the can and opened the windows for ventilation and avoided the freshly painted room for a couple of days. You probably figured these were adequate precautions. But the toxins in VOCs can linger and linger and linger. Unfortunately, research on the adverse affects of formaldehyde shows that we would be better off trying to keep it out of the home in the first place.

The following chart lists a few other chemicals that are often embedded in man-made products. Note where they are apt to be found and what they may be able to do to the body.

WHAT TO DO?

It's obviously impossible to banish all these chemicals and synthetics from the home. They are built into the manufacture of computers and computer accessories, cell phones, televisions. They're in just about every gadget and product intended to improve the quality of our life and lifestyle. But it is possible to be vigilant and learn more about dangerous chemicals that could make their way into the home. In the Appendix you will find lists of top-notch organizations and books that provide valuable information to help you protect your home and your family.

When we are educated about dangerous pollutants we can make informed choices to limit their presence in the home. We can even use safer alternatives that are already on the market.

Finally, remember the essential truth of holism. All creation is interconnected, interdependent, and divine. We are better off when surrounded by nature rather than synthetics, which are not biodegradable and end up in landfills that mar the earth. When we protect ourselves, we protect the environment. On a deeper level, when we honor and respect the environment, we honor and respect ourselves.

Recycle, Recreate, Renovate!

We can also honor nature in the home and help sustain the environment by participating in a smart new method of recycling—reusing materials whenever possible. Many companies now sell products created from reclaimed wood instead of newly harvested lumber. Whether you need a frame to hold up a house or a frame to hold a painting, it is possible to protect precious trees by choosing reclaimed wood.

It isn't always necessary to buy beautiful objects for the home. Seek out treasures from the world of nature. On your next hike through the woods or stroll along the beach, bring back a natural memento. Create a collection of found organic objects to celebrate your personal experiences and appreciation

CHEMICAL CHART

Chemical	Common Uses	Health Effects
Benzene	solvent once commonly used in paints, plastics, rubber, dyes, detergents; present in tobacco smoke	carcinogen neurotoxin irritating to eyes and skin may cause fetal damage may disrupt normal cell function
Trichloroethylene	solvent used in paint strippers, adhesives, spot removers, and rug cleaners	neurotoxin may cause fetal damage possible carcinogen
Phthalates	soft vinyl used in shower curtains, wall coverings, flooring, furniture, toys, and clothing such as raincoats; also used as an additive in paints and wood finishes	may harm reproductive and immune system linked to childhood asthma and some other respiratory problems possible carcinogen
Organotin compounds	heat and light stabilizer used in food packing materials, glass coating, polyurethane foam, and PVC pipes	may disrupt hormonal and reproductive systems may harm immune system
Polybrominated diphenyl ethers (PBDEs)	flame retardants added to mattresses, carpets, furniture foam, and textiles; used in wiring in electronic products	neurotoxin may mimic hormones may be carcinogenic
Alkylphenol ethoxylates	synthetics often found in laundry detergent, textiles, leather, paints, all-purpose cleaners, spot removers, and disinfectants	may disrupt hormonal system believed to mimic estrogen, causing sexual development problems

SAFER OPTIONS

* Planning to paint a room? Select zero-VOC or low-VOC paints.

* Refinishing furniture or staining a floor? Choose nontoxic varnishes and stains.

* Swap synthetic carpets for biodegradable area rugs-these are also easier to clean.

* Use candles free of artificial scent.

* Avoid commercial air fresheners; make little sachets of baking soda or natural potpourri using cheesecloth tied with silk ribbon.

* Open the windows and air out your home for a few minutes each day. Make this a healthy ritual.

* Make your own household cleansers; they're easy to create and affordable. Here are three recipes to start with:

All-purpose Cleanser

2 tablespoons distilled white vinegar

1 teaspoon baking soda

2 cups water

1 or 2 drops of a favorite essential oil (optional, for fragrance)

Combine all ingredients in a spray bottle and use for general cleaning.

Furniture and Floor Polish

¼ cup olive oil

2 tablespoons lemon juice

1 or 2 drops of a favorite essential oil (optional, for fragrance)

Mix the ingredients well and apply with a rag to keep finished wood shining.

Glass Cleaner

⅛ cup distilled white vinegar

1 cup water

Combine all ingredients in a spray bottle and use for cleaning glass. Use old newspaper to wipe the glass to avoid streaking.

of the environment. Let it bring out the artist that exists within you.

Look at the way that the designer Clodagh has established an arresting display and bridge between the dining room and living room on the following pages. An artist retrieved the piece of wood, nature's discard, and manipulated it into a stunning sculpture that becomes a powerful yet serene focal point.

Organic art is always mysterious and surprising. And if we simply let nature inspire us, even the act of meal preparation can reveal lovely objects. Consider the contents of the wooden bowl at right, placed on a window seat in the artist's home in western New York. Aren't the onion skins beautiful?

And, of course, it is still possible to recycle the old-fashioned way. Give unwanted objects to someone else or hold a garage sale. Poke through flea markets, garage sales, second-hand stores, and antique shops for that special something— a beautiful old metal frame (instead of a new plastic one), a handsome cupboard with authentic age (rather than a new cupboard with a fake distressed surface), a cotton braid rug woven by someone's grandmother. A vintage object may not be new, but it bears the stamp of history and it is new to its new caretaker.

There is something wonderful about reusing objects that were discarded by

someone or that fell to the side of a path in the woods or were left behind by a wave on the sand. That act of reclamation participates in the cycle that accompanies all existence. We pick up an object and preserve it just a bit longer before it moves on to its natural phase of destruction and decomposition.

Nature in the Home:
The Healing Force

Nature is our ally, and natural products have a positive effect on our well-being. We notice the imperfect details in organic products, and since all creation is imperfect, these add to the charm—the sumptuous yet uneven color of the vegetable dyes used for an area rug or a hand-made dhurrie; the imperfect surface on a piece of wheel-thrown terra-cotta pottery; the seashells and sea glass that reflect the ebb and flow of the tides. When we sit in a room filled with such lovely objects that reflect the natural environment, the jumbled thoughts that rattle around in the mind settle down. We know, instinctively, that the appreciation of nature is an expression of appreciation for the deeper self.

What is the most effective way to introduce nature so it feels organic, truly connected to the décor, rather than like an accessory or randomly placed object? Use the visual clues on display in every natural environment—nature always gets it right. Organize organic products so that they highlight nature's earthy colors, textures, and shapes.

Notice how the following designers and architects seamlessly introduce nature into the interiors shown on the following pages. A couple of the rooms are lavish; most are modest and unassuming. But they all celebrate nature. And in each one, we consistently feel nature's presence, whether it's built into the design or added to the décor.

LEFT: Home detail by Susanka.

RIGHT: Straw bale home dining area by Kelly Lerner and Peter Gang.

PAGES 134-135:

LEFT: Sitting room by Susanka.

RIGHT: Living room by Clodagh.

LEFT AND ABOVE: With Gaia
Design kitchen and living room.

PLANTS-CULTIVATE YOUR GREEN THUMB

Finally, an open invitation to nature should extend to living, breathing plants. Many people keep plants out of their home, insisting that they kill them, no matter what they do. Often what they do is ignore the plants and expect them to fend for themselves. People with hectic lives sometimes think of plants as yet one more challenge—one more thing to care for when time is already stretched far too thin.

But considering plants a bother does more harm than we realize. Numerous studies have proven that houseplants are worth their weight in gold, something that the ancient Vedic scholars realized long ago. Plants have the power to lower stress and blood pressure. They have the power to improve the ability to concentrate and increase productivity. And they improve the quality of the air inside the home.

In the past 30 years, research has shown that popular varieties of durable houseplants, even the inexpensive ones that are sold in supermarkets, are easy to grow and remove some of the dangerous VOCs that contaminate indoor air. Small openings in the leaves of these green plants, along with microorganisms that live in the soil near their roots, break down some of the harmful organic chemicals found in formaldehyde, benzene, and trichloroethylene.

This metabolic process, which supplies the plant's root system with oxygen, converts harmful chemicals into a food source for these detoxifying houseplants while purifying the air. According to experiments conducted by NASA and the Associated Landscape Contractors of America and described in the report "Interior Landscape Plants for Indoor Air Pollution Abatement" (1989), it takes just three hardworking leafy plants in eight-to-ten-inch pots per hundred square feet to eliminate a significant percentage of the VOCs in the surrounding air.

Some other houseplants, such as aloe (Aloe barbadensis), have medicinal properties that have been appreciated for hundreds of years.

The juice from the majestic aloe, which is often called the first-aid plant, soothes cuts and burns, including sunburns. Aloe also softens the skin, as do the crushed petals and leaves of violets. Many herbs, such as mint and lemon balm, can be grown indoors and brewed into healthy teas.

MAKE PLANTS MEMORABLE

Many people tell me they like the idea of plants but simply don't know how to take care of them. If this reflects your experience, just remember these few guidelines to give your plants a healthy start. Most plants that we purchase are stuck inside plastic containers. Repot them in any natural product, such as terra-cotta. Then consider their world of origin. Succulents, which retain water in their leaves,

ABOVE: Aloe.

LEFT: Mindful placement by Kinari Design.

BENEFICIAL HOUSEGUESTS

Common Name	Bamboo palm	Dracaena Janet Craig	Madagascar dragon tree	Peace Lily
Scientific Name	Chamaedorea seifrizii	Dracaena deremensis	Dracaena marginata	Spathiphyllum
Common Name	Snake plant	Golden pothos	English Ivy	
Scientific Name	Sansevieria trifasciata	Epipremnum aureum	Hedera helix	

thrive in dry soil under a hot sun. They're not happy when they're repeatedly flooded with water or stuck inside a shady room. On the other hand, leafy greens and ferns, including most of the plants in the list at left, come from the tropics or forests. They prefer a rich, moist soil and filtered light that replicates the light that peeks through the forest's thick canopy of trees.

And the solution for the problem of benign neglect? Just play against your weakness. Instead of placing individual plants randomly-one in this corner of a room, another on a side table near a window, a third on the bureau in a bedroom—group them together on their own low table or directly on the floor. If they share the same needs, put them together in a huge planter. The cluster will mimic their appearance in nature. And while each solitary plant may have been easy to overlook in the past, grouped together they will become a distinctive display that makes you notice them and their individuality. You will see the diversity expressed in their leaves, hues, and unique patterns of growth.

Some larger plants, such as the pencil cactus shown in the loft photo at right, look positively statuesque standing alone. Standing by the burnished silver metal door and show-cased by the natural light from the huge sky-light, this cactus is impossible to overlook. Clodagh, the designer of this handsome loft, has also framed the cactus between two

massive pillars, which accentuates its presence in the room. She has transformed a lovely plant, which expresses the beauty of nature, into a living work of art.

By organizing your plants meaningfully, so that they express their beauty, you will notice them and take care of them. And they will show their appreciation by growing robust and bringing calm to the home.

In the end, we pay a price when we underestimate the power of nature's presence inside the home. We feel nature's presence; we feel nature's absence. The former feels good; the latter feels wrong—viscerally. Intuitively, the body and mind know that nature's presence is essential if the home is to become an oasis, an authentic sanctuary.

Imagine stepping into the appealing entryway on pages 142 to 143 in an artist's straw bale home in western New York, or imagine catching a glimpse of this area while sitting in the adjoining living room.

Everything on display in the entryway is organic: the weathered ladder leaning against the wall, the handmade felt artwork above the Tibetan medicine cabinet, each basket tucked high in a corner. Even the composition of the straw bale walls releases the positive power of nature. In a world fraught with tension and stress, we all need to take positive advantage of nature. We should follow this artist's example and let nature surround and inspire us in the home, where it can provide much-needed peace.

ABOVE: Loft entrance by Clodagh.

PAGES 142 TO 143: Western New York home.

When your heart speaks
take good notes.
–Judith Hamel

WHAT DREW YOU TO BE AN ARCHITECT OR DESIGNER?

"I loved everything spatial from the time I was a small child. I used to love to hang upside down on a chair and imagine myself walking on the ceiling. It would shift my world. I've always wanted to explore space in every possible way."

–SARAH SUSANKA, SUSANKA STUDIOS

"When I was young, I loved the instruments of the trade-squares, triangles, rulers. I loved using them and creating lines, even when I couldn't do this very well. Now, most of us don't use these tools. But I have hung on to the greater meaning of architecture: shaping small or large or private or urban spaces with a strong sense of social sensibility. I can't imagine spending my time doing anything else."

–BRUNO BONDANELLI, DESIGNX

"I was always interested in colors and textures. And I realized that a well-designed space could alter my mood. It could make me feel like I was in another time and place."

–KIM NADEL, NICHE ENVIRONMENTALLY SMART DESIGN GROUP

"An imagination that wasn't matched by my budget drew me to become a designer. I can't possibly change my own house every time I get a new idea, so I enjoy working on other people's homes. Also, I love to hear clients say how much they love living in a space that I've helped them create. This is a positive feeling that never wears off."

–DOUG ATHERLEY, KINARI DESIGN

"I have always been involved in design and the creative arts. I had a natural talent and eye for design and simply enjoyed it. I was finally drawn to study architecture after my daughter was born. Her birth and new life inspired me to embark on a journey to create healthy, beautiful environments. I've been enjoying this ever since."

–MARY GORDON, GAIATECTURE DESIGN STUDIO

"I was young, just 15, when I finished high school in Ireland. My parents wanted me to go to a university and do something with math or sciences. But I wasn't keen to go in that direction. Then, just before I turned sixteen, I broke my back. As I lay on the ground, I looked up

and saw a sign that said, why not become a fashion designer? I liked that idea. I studied fashion for a short while and quickly created a successful business. Years later, I ended up in Spain. I decided to learn Spanish while I fixed up a huge farm, with its houses, and discovered this is what I really love to do."
—CLODAGH, CLODAGH DESIGN

"When I heard Maharishi Mahesh Yogi talk about natural building, these words captured my attention: 'We build in a way where everything nourishes everything.' In that moment, I relived my building career. The only part of my homes in alignment with this principle was the timber frame. The rest I knew was toxic. In an instant I had a picture in my mind of dead fish in the water. I saw a pipe leading into the water dumping green stuff that kills the fish. I saw that the pipe connected to a factory making building materials that are destroying the ecosystem. This was the end of my career as a conventional builder. It was eight months before I built again— in clay, straw, and timber—practicing that law of nature where everything nourishes everything."
—ROBERT LAPORTE, ECONEST

"We build green to reduce our impact on the environment. We also like working with natural materials, as they are often lower impact. Conventional fabricated building materials are so consistent. Earth plasters and adobe floors, even finely crafted, have a range of textural and visual details, from subtle undulations in the walls down to small variations in the floor. This emulates the quality of the natural world and gives a home a softness and interest more commonly found outside."
—SUSIE HARRINGTON AND KALEN JONES, WITH GAIA DESIGN

"I like to make beautiful, useful things that enhance the experiences of everyday life. I was a potter before I became an architect, and I think of houses as vessels for living. I love working with the jigsaw puzzle of people, materials, and the natural elements of sun, wind, water, and landscape to craft a home that reflects all of their unique personalities."
—KELLY LERNER, ONE WORLD DESIGN

There is no mystery in the art of design. Every design decision sets in motion a predictable, predetermined consequence.

CHAPTER FIVE:
The Defining Details—Make Them Matter

The defining details in interior décor lock in the ambience that, as discussed in Chapter Two ("Function and Ambience–Match Them Up"), should reinforce a room's intended use. Just as the presence of nature adds emotional warmth to a house or apartment, so do defining details. But defining details create this warmth by injecting your unique personality into the décor.

The successful choice of defining details serves as a reminder of who we are and what we love. They reconnect us to the heart of what matters. A treasured box of pebbles collected from hikes over the years commemorates those times when we explored the beauty of the natural world; the paintings on the walls celebrate our appreciation of the creativity of the human mind and hand; the personal photographs grouped together on a table trigger thoughts of loved ones who enrich our lives.

All these defining details, which should be displayed to catch the eye, speak to the soul and help to put life in perspective. Looking at what you love, you may find your thoughts slowly turning away from the work piled up on the desk or the long list of tasks you think you need to do. An authentic home, with its well-chosen and well-placed defining details, changes the focus and encourages relaxation. This is the power of defining details: They remind us of our special essence and turn our home into a uniquely reassuring and comforting space, a place where we know we belong.

The addition of defining details to any room is generally the final step in the design process, and it often presents an enormous challenge. So many of my clients have told me that they just end up putting mementos and other special objects on any available surface. They see a space and fill it. As for artwork, photographs, and other personal treasures that they want to hang on a wall, they feel insecure about what should go where.

Many of them insist that they lack a creative eye. I have heard some variant of the following sentence so many times: "I just don't have the flair for organizing art or photos or my collection of _____."

But success in this endeavor has nothing to do with innate creativity. Success comes from thinking correctly about the meaning of the objects to be put on display. Once you understand the pivotal role they play in helping turn a house or apartment into a powerfully supportive home, you can shift your design methodology. No longer will you blindly hang artwork on a wall and aimlessly park free-standing objects in any available slot on a table or a shelf. You will know how to display defining details so they add their positive power to your home.

The Law of Cause and Effect

The Vedic scholars expressed the concept of cause and effect in their own spiritual philosophy as karma. They saw that for every action, there is a specific reaction (something Newton observed thousands of years later). They believed that this law governs all human action and thought; on a more mundane level, they observed that it covers the design of buildings and interiors.

These scholars saw in their own creation of structures that every design decision led to a predictable consequence experienced by the human body. In other words, when creating a home and determining the look of its interior, we feel the consequences of each choice in the body, mind, and soul. It is important to be deeply mindful of everything we do, because each decision sets in motion the law of cause and effect.

The need for mindfulness assumes great importance if we expect to create a home that really connects to each of us. Let me draw a parallel: When you put on lipstick or shave your face in the morning, you carefully watch what you are doing. If your mind and eyes wander off, you know (probably from experience) that there is a good chance you will get lipstick on more than your lips or nick yourself. During this act of personal grooming, you stay mindfully engaged. It is important to be equally mindful during each step of the design process.

Clutter–Define It, Consign It

Many of us pick up too many objects on impulse. We see something appealing and buy it. But visual allure may be the extent of that object's appeal; it may not truly connect to us. Each time something meaningless is added to our décor and home, ultimately we demean ourselves.

This may seem like an overstatement, but the presence of an insignificant object in a room becomes a distraction that diminishes the positive power of the important place that is a home. It also takes up valuable space, becoming a perfect example of that confusing thing called clutter.

Clutter is a source of mystery to so many people. Often, clients tell me they just don't know how to deal with it; it grows uncontrollably, like bacteria in a petri dish. But I've noticed that the real problem for most people is not dealing with clutter, but defining it. Most people don't know what it is.

So what is clutter? Think back to the Vedic law of nature that asserts that there is nothing random in the grand design of the universe. Now think about your home, your private universe. Just as there is nothing random in the design of the universe, there should be nothing random in the design or organization of your home. This is a helpful way to identify clutter: If you see an object anywhere in your home that doesn't serve a utilitarian function or that doesn't connect to who you are or what you love, this object is random.

Randomness leads to superficiality; superficiality sows the seeds of clutter. Physical clutter leads to mental clutter. Mental clutter elevates stress. By avoiding randomness, you can eliminate clutter, lower stress, and create an authentic, truly calming home—an oasis.

The meaningless or random object in a room reinforces the point that every design decision, even the introduction of a seemingly inconsequential object into the décor, has predictable consequences. A meaningless object fails to trigger thoughts that connect to us. It inspires, at best, a neutral response, which, remember, is a negative response, since neutral does nothing positive. And a negative response slyly brings down our mood.

Choosing Furniture and Furnishings

Furniture and furnishings are also defining details in the home—larger versions of the decorative objects on display. It is important to select them based on the needs and preferences of the human body, a pivotal vastu guideline discussed in Chapter One, "Design to Please the Human Body." Let's learn about some of the predictable consequences attached to furniture choices and examine the ways designers use these consequences to advantage.

The Power of the Square

As I discussed earlier, the height and breadth of the human form, with arms outstretched, fits into a perfect square—perfect because its sides are fixed and equal. The symmetrical form of the square symbolizes the Vedic view of the celestial realm, an expression of harmony and balance.

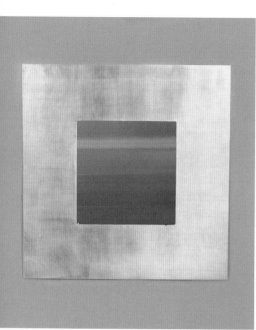

The energy of the square is static and unmoving. Square-based shapes are grounding, calming. This is why mandalas, Buddhist and Hindu meditation aids, are typically drawn in a square; if they include a circle, its circumference is bordered by a square. When people meditate on the mandala, they fix their eyes on its center point to still the mind and concentrate on their spiritual practice.

The Power of the Circle

The circular form of the earth is full of energy and movement. Circles and ovals, unlike squares, are dynamic. Circles are in constant motion—they exhibit the properties of the wheel. When presented with a circle or circular object, the eyes tend to follow its circumference, or rim; they are disinclined to focus on the center. See for yourself at left.

Squares and Circles as Defining Details

Since squares and rectangles represent static energy, they tend to serve as anchors in a room. When we sit at a square or rectangular dining table, we tend to relax and eat more slowly, which is good for the digestive system. We are apt to linger awhile, which leads to a more convivial experience. Working at a square or rectangular desk can actually improve productivity because the shape of its surface helps focus our thoughts.

Since circles and ovals trigger movement, they tend to animate us. The circular bed was a commercial disaster because people could never orient their bodies on the round mattress; the result was restlessness, not sleep. The dynamic energy of the circle also explains why we rarely see circular mirrors in a bathroom. The round shape makes it hard to focus on the face when applying makeup or shaving.

A circular or oval dining table tends to inspire brisk talk and actions. We are apt to eat more quickly, and the conversation is usually more spirited and lively. This is why circular or oval tables are ideal for conference rooms. The shape of the table encourages brainstorming and the rigorous flow of ideas.

If you like the look of a circular dining table for your home, you can preserve the rituals that ought to accompany meal time and help people to eat slowly by anchoring down the energy. Place a square-based rug on the floor or use square place mats or a square table cloth. Notice how Doug Atherley, founder of Kinari Design in London, grounds the energy created by the circular table in the dining area of this multipurpose room. He places rectangular mirrors, with a pair of matching cubes, against one wall and displays a pair of rectangular hangings on another nearby wall. These additions introduce the calm that dominates the ambience.

ABOVE LEFT: Square.

LOWER LEFT: Circle.

RIGHT AND PAGES 152 TO 153:
Living and dining room by Kinari Design.

ABOVE AND RIGHT: Kinari Design.

The Power of Asymmetry and Symmetry

When choosing furniture and considering its placement in a room, it is also necessary to take into account the power of asymmetry and symmetry. While the overall human form represents a perfect square, which is aligned symmetrically, the details of the body—eyes, ears, lips, any feature that comes in pairs-are slightly asymmetrical. In addition, the body tends to assume asymmetrical positions; it should come as no surprise that we feel more comfortable when we sit in spaces where the furniture is arranged asymmetrically.

The body's preference for asymmetry doesn't mean that symmetry should be banished from the home—to the contrary. Just be mindful of choosing symmetry or asymmetry when arranging furniture and other defining details in a room. As always, consider the function of the room and its appropriate ambience; remember that whatever placement is chosen will lead to predetermined consequences experienced by the body.

Look at the dreamy ambience in this bedroom at right which was designed by Clodagh. Everything in this pretty space is symmetrically arranged, right down to the slim vases embedded in the bedposts, with their matching flowers. This symmetry is grounding and creates a powerful feeling of tranquility that is perfect for this private space.

The bedroom on page 156 was designed by Bruno Bondanelli, the founder of Designx. This room, which was created for a Hollywood couple, is unabashedly lavish, but its opulence also expresses the calm that accompanies symmetry. The rich colors of the raw silk fabrics, with the black band of silk that binds them, are mirrored in the swirling hues of the wool carpet on the hardwood floor. The symmetrical placement and cohesive palette create the harmony that belongs in every bedroom.

The final image on page 157 shows a modest reading area in a bedroom designed by Linda Spence, the founder of L. Y. Spence

ABOVE AND RIGHT: Bedroom designed by Clodagh.

How is your body positioned right now as you read this book? Are you sitting in a chair with your back ramrod straight, knees uncrossed, and your feet placed side by side on the floor, or are you curled up in a chair or lying casually on a bed? In the course of the next couple of days, notice where you choose to sit when you enter a room. Do you ever sit in the dead center of an empty sofa? Is your sitting posture ever perfect enough that you could balance this book on your head? Now examine the arrangement of the furnishings in your home. Is the organization mostly symmetrical? Do you see and feel the formality in this alignment? Remember, these defining details create the comfort level in a house or apartment.

Designs in California. The furniture is asymmetrically placed near the corner of the room to create a cozy area that appeals to the body and suits the purpose of the space. The symmetrical placement of the statues of the Buddha in the recessed cutout in the wall adds tranquility, while the asymmetrical placement of the table display, with its defining details, establishes a gentle rhythm. The total effect is personal, nourishing, and quietly mindful.

The Power of Rhythm and Flow

Occasionally, we want a collection of similar objects to make a single unified statement. Perhaps we want people to admire a row of blue spice jars in a kitchen or a shelf filled with wicker baskets. But more often we want our guests to notice the defining details of each object in a collection. An asymmetrical arrangement of these objects is more likely to achieve this goal. Asymmetry creates visual flow, encourages the eyes to move from object to object.

LEFT: Hollywood bedroom by Designx.

RIGHT: Reading area by L.Y. Spence Designs.

The Power of Three

The power of three is acknowledged throughout the world. The number three corresponds to the trinity in Christianity and the three primary gods in Hinduism. Three speaks of creation, preservation, and destruction. Three primary colors, red, blue, and yellow, reveal our visible world. Many parts of the human body subscribe to the rule of three. There are three layers to the skin (epidermis, dermis, and hypodermis), three parts to the ear (inner, middle, and outer), and three types of deciduous teeth (incisors, canines, and molars).

ABOVE AND RIGHT: Thoughtful placement by Kinari Design.

FAR RIGHT: L.Y. Spence Designs: Predictable consequences.

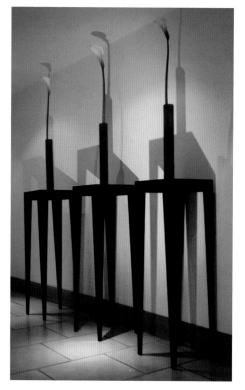

Freud's theory of human psychology is based on the id, ego, and superego. Aristotle unified time, place, and action. An ancient proverb is associated with three wise monkeys that remind us to hear no evil, speak no evil, and see no evil. And just imagine if Julius Caesar had said "veni, vici" (I came, I conquered) instead of "veni, vidi, vici" (I came, I saw, I conquered). It's doubtful that we would remember the shorter phrase. Two words linked together lack the power of three.

So when you are placing your defining details in each room of your home, remember that three objects placed on a surface or a wall are more engaging to the eye than two. Notice how this display designed by Doug Atherley creates asymmetry, movement, and power.

By contrast, defining details grouped in even numbers—in particular, two or four objects—have the same effect as square based objects and symmetrical arrangements. They draw our eyes to the center of the display. We are less inclined to take in the defining details.

Examine the following series of interior tableaux, which were created by the designer Linda Spence. See how your eye reacts when she uses symmetry and asymmetry, circles and squares, odd and even numbers. Notice how each set of choices focuses your attention. The predictable consequences that accompany each of these displays create a similar visceral and visual reaction in all of us. There is no mystery in design.

The Power of Cohesion

By observing the law of cause and effect in choosing defining details, we introduce cohesion into the home. Walking from room to room or area to area, we feel these defining details, along with the healthy presence of nature, act as a quiet yet tangible expression of the holism that resonates deeply within all of us.

Defining details—the circle and the square, odd and even numbers, movement and stillness, symmetry and asymmetry—also reflect the dualities that create the rhythms governing our world. And just as dualities bring order to the universe, the meaningful use of dualities brings order, harmony, and comfort into the home.

Let's look at one final interior environment and see how everything in the décor fits together, like the pages in a book or the notes in a musical composition. This Hollywood duplex on pages 161 to 167, tucked behind its modern exterior and minimalist entryway, was created by Bruno Bondanelli of Designx.

Every one of Bruno's design decisions makes positive use of the critical matters of space discussed in this book. The outside makes its presence felt inside: Sunlight pours through the skylight, the huge bank of windows, and the sliding doors to the interior courtyard and side patio. Nature is honored in the preference for organic materials and by the presence of the tropical plants indoors and out. Even the two dominant colors in the interior, green and brown, reflect nature's

positive power. Notice how the warmth of the dark wood floor is mirrored in the warm reds in the painting on the wall. The placement of this bold painting cleverly shifts the focus away from the flat-screen TV. In its every detail, this duplex demonstrates the power of space used to positive advantage.

We've come to the end of a journey that has invited us to rethink our understanding of the meaning of the authentic home and our understanding of the critical matters of space, with a bit of homespun advice. By observing these five guidelines, which are based on the ancient wisdom of vastu, we see, through the lovely work of the architects and designers showcased in this book, that we can empower ourselves once we know how to use personal space to our advantage.

A dream home doesn't have to remain elusive. You can transform your apartment or house, bungalow or loft, whether modest or grand, into a meaningful, authentic home that celebrates yourself and your glorious world. All that is needed is reverence for our holistic relationship with nature and the desire to celebrate our unique essence. If we stay focused on these two objectives, our home will, most assuredly, quiet the mind, warm the heart, and soothe the soul.

RIGHT: Home designed by Designx.

PAGE 163: Entryway.

PUTTING IT ALL TOGETHER

1. *Design to please the human body.* The heart and soul tell us how to proceed when creating a home. They should take the lead in design, not the eyes.

2. *Function and ambience—match them up.* Nothing exists in isolation, and everything that exists should serve a valuable purpose and function. The intended design of every created object honors this rule.

3. *Light and shadow—welcome their dance.* Everything that exists has an opposing force, and these dualities enrich our appreciation of the world. After all, how can we enjoy the sunlight unless we experience the darkness of night?

4. *The healing touch of nature—aim for organic.* Celebrate your interconnection with nature by bringing it into the home. Let its power and quiet beauty inspire you.

5. *The defining details—make them matter.* There is no mystery in the art of design. Every decision sets in motion a predictable, predetermined consequence.

LEFT, RIGHT, AND PAGE 166:
Views of duplex living room.

PAGE 167: Duplex courtyard.

APPENDIX

Designers and Architects

Clodagh Design
Clodagh
New York, New York
212-780-5300
www.clodagh.com
info@clodagh.com

Designx
Bruno Bondanelli
Los Angeles, California
323-653-1218
www.designx-architecture.com
info@designx-architecture.com

EcoNest
Paula Baker-Laporte and Robert Laporte
Tesuque, New Mexico
505-989-1813
www.econest.com
info@econest.com
EcoNest also conducts workshops and
seminars, and offers an apprenticeship
program in ecological home-building to
promising individuals. Contact EcoNest
for further details.

Gaiatecture Design Studio
Mary Golden
Honeoye Falls, New York
585-624-2540
www.gaiatecture.com
gaiatecture@hotmail.com

Kinari Design
Doug Atherley
London, United Kingdom
U.S.: 917-714-3310
U.K.: 44-207-221-0082
www.kinaridesign.com
info@kinaridesign.com

L. Y. Spence Designs
Linda Spence
Foster City, California
650-573-1147
www.LYSpenceDesigns.com
LSpenceDsn@aol.com

**NICHE environmentally
smart design group**
Kim Nadel
Brooklyn, New York
718-832-7274
www.design-niche.com
info@design-niche.com

One World Design
Kelly Lerner
Spokane, Washington
509-838-8812
www.one-world-design.com
One World also conducts seminars
and workshops on greening your home,
straw bale and sustainable design,
and eco-remodeling. Visit
www.naturalremodeling.com for details.

Susanka Studios
Sarah Susanka
Raleigh, North Carolina
www.notsobighouse.com
ssusanka@notsobighouse.com

thread collective
Gita Nandan, Mark Mancuso, Elliott Maltby
Brooklyn, New York
718-389-1852
www.threadcollective.com

With Gaia Design
Susie Harrington and Kalen Jones
Moab, Utah
435-259-7073
www.withgaia.com
info@withgaia.com

Vastu Living
Kathleen Cox
New York, New York
917-848-0495
www.vastuliving.com
info@vastuliving.com

Designer Product Lines

**The Clodagh Collection and
Clodagh Design Signature**
Visit www.clodagh.com to view Clodagh's
furniture showroom, product design, and
licensing division or contact
info@clodagh.com or 212-780-5300.

Niche Shape
Visit www.design-niche.com to view
Kim Nadel's collection of furniture created
from reclaimed materials or contact
info@design-niche.com or 718-832-7274.

Designers' Books

By Clodagh:
*Total Design: Contemplate, Cleanse,
Clarify, and Create Your Personal Spaces*
(Clarkson Potter, 2001)

By Kelly Lerner:
*Natural Remodeling for the Not-So-Green
House: Bringing Your Home into Harmony
with Nature* (Lark Books, 2006)

**By Paula Baker-Laporte and
Robert Laporte:**
*EcoNest: Creating Sustainable Sanctuaries
of Clay, Straw, and Timber* (Gibbs Smith,
2005)

**By Paula Baker-Laporte, Erica Elliot,
and John Banta:**
*Prescriptions for A Healthy House: A
Practical Guide for Architects, Builders &
Homeowners* (New Society Publishers, 2001)

By Sarah Susanka:
*The Not So Big House: A Blueprint for the
Way We Really Live* (Taunton Press, 1998)

*Creating the Not So Big House: Insights
and Ideas for the New American Home*
(Taunton Press, 2002) *Not So Big
Solutions for Your Home* (Taunton Press,
2002) *Home by Design: Transforming
Your House into Home* (Taunton Press,
2004) *Inside the Not So Big House:
Discovering the Details That Bring a
Home to Life* (Taunton Press, 2005)
*Outside the Not So Big House: Creating
the Landscape of Home* (Newtown, The
Taunton Press, 2006) *The Not So Big Life:
Making Room for What Really Matters*
(New York, Random House, 2007)

By Kathleen Cox:
Vastu Living: Creating a Home for the Soul
(Marlowe & Company, 2000) *The Power of
Vastu Living: Welcoming Your Soul into Your
Home and Workplace* (Atria, 2002)

Designer Recommendations

FROM CLODAGH:

Serpentine Studio
(wall finishes and paintings)
Louise Crandell
New York, New York
212-674-7235
serpentinenyc@aol.com

Jeffrey Aronoff
(throws and upholstery fabric)
New York, New York
518-671-6501
www.jeffreyaronoff.com
handwovenhudson@aol.com

Tony Conway
(photo-based paintings)
Senior & Shopmaker Gallery
New York, New York
212-213-6767
www.seniorandshopmaker.com
gallery@seniorandshopmaker.com

FROM DESIGNX:

Universal Hardwood
(sustainable, recycled hardwood
and bamboo flooring)
Los Angeles, California
310-839-9663
www.universalwood.com
universalwood@adelphia.net

Livingreen
(environmentally-friendly building
materials and furnishings)
Santa Barbara, California
866-966-1319
www.livingreen.com
info@livingreen.com

Greenopia
(guide to eco-friendly retailers, services,
and organizations in Los Angeles)
Santa Monica, California
310-917-1100
www.greenopia.com

FROM ECONEST:

Eco-terric
(healthy, natural products for the home
and its occupants)
Bozeman, Montana
866-582-7547
www.eco-terric.com
info@eco-terric.com

Planetary Solutions
(healthy building materials from flooring,
counters, and tiles to carpeting, linoleum,
and paints)
Boulder, Colorado
303-442-6228
www.planetearth.com

Janice's
(chemically-free, natural fiber mattresses,
bedding, and linens and personal-care and
home-care products)
800-526-4237
www.janices.com

FROM GAIATECTURE DESIGN STUDIOS:

Tactile Interiors
(designers and installers of nontoxic wall
finishes, specializing in natural plasters)
Yorkville, California
707-895-2028
www.tactileinc.com
inquiries@tactileinc.com

Hartmut R Deeg,
master cabinet maker
(custom cabinetry and fine furniture)
Klassic International Furniture, Inc.
Honeoye Falls, New York
585-624-2540
hrdeeg@gmail.com

Sharon Kissack
(felt maker, quilt maker, creator of paper
collages, and assembler of objects)
Rochester, New York
585-624-4083
skissack@frontiernet.net

FROM KINARI DESIGN:

Hiran Mitra
(Indian painter)
Represented by Art Border Line
London, United Kingdom
44-203-238-2004
www.artborderline.com
contact@artborderline.com

Paint & Paper Library
(creators of paints and wallpapers)
London, United Kingdom
(also distributed in the U.S.)
44-207-823-7755
www.paintlibrary.co.uk
info@paintlibrary.co.uk

Wabi Art
(contemporary Japanese art)
London, United Kingdom
44-778-601-2224
www.wabiart.com
yumi@wabiart.com

FROM L. Y. SPENCE DESIGNS:

Vetrazzo
(recycled glass turned into one-of-a-kind surfaces)
Richmond, California
510-234-5550
www.vetrazzo.com
info@vetrazzo.com

Sandhill Industries
(tiles made of all recycled glass)
Boise, Idaho
208-345-6508
www.sandhillind.com
sales@sandhillind.com

Kirei Board
(manufacturer of wood substitute made
from the sorghum plant)
San Diego, California
619-236-9924
www.kireiusa.com
info@kireiusa.com

FROM NICHE:

Odegard
(socially-responsible producer of hand-tufted,
nontreated silk and wool rugs)
New York, New York
212-545-0069
www.odegardinc.com

Innovations
(environmentally-sound wall coverings, such
as Innvironments Cork)
New York, NY
800-227-8053
www.innovationsusa.com

Tucker Robbins
(former monk, now designer of home
furnishings, such as mortar stools created by
Asian village craftsmen)
718-764-0222
Long Island City, New York
www.tuckerrobbins.com

FROM ONE WORLD DESIGN:

Yolo Colorhouse
(eco-friendly paints)
Portland, Oregon
503-493-8275
www.yolocolorhouse.com
info@yolocolorhouse.com

Paperstone by KlipTech Composites
(eco-friendly composite for countertops,
tables, floor tiles, wall covering)
Hoquiam, Washington
360-538-9815
www.kliptech.com

Marmoleum by Forbo Flooring
(for flooring and other surfaces-made with
natural materials and installed with solvent-
free adhesives)
Hazleton, Pennsylvania
800-842-7839
www.forbolinoleumna.com
info@fL-NA.com

FROM thread collective:

Bonded Logic Ultratouch
(nontoxic, natural cotton fiber insulation)
Chandler, Arizona
480-812-9114
www.bondedlogic.com
sales@bondedlogic.com

IceStone
(durable surfaces made from recycled glass
and cement)
Brooklyn, New York
718-624-4900
www.icestone.biz
info@icestone.biz

Plyboo by Smith & Fong Company
(eco-friendly bamboo flooring, paneling,
veneer, and plywood)
South San Francisco, California
866-835-9859
www.plyboo.com
sales@plyboo.com

FROM WITH GAIA DESIGN:

Environmental Building News
(online database of green materials)
Brattleboro, Vermont
802-257-7300
www.buildinggreen.com
info@buildinggreen.com

FROM KATHLEEN COX:

www.healthychild.org
website that advocates healthy environments
for children, with information about keeping
the home safe from pollutants

www.treehugger.com
Internet magazine founded by Graham Hill to provide the latest on environmentally responsible products, info, and resources

www.novica.com
Arts and crafts by artists and artisans worldwide; sales directly support them and their work

Additional Reading

Daniel D. Chiras, *The Natural House: A Complete Guide to Healthy, Energy-efficient, Environmental Homes* (Chelsea Green, 2000) Joseph F. Kennedy, Michael Smith, and Catherine Wanek (editors), *The Art of Natural Building: Design, Construction, Resources* (New Society Publishers, 2002) Ted Owens, *Building with Awareness: The Construction of a Hybrid Home*, DVD and guidebook (Syncronos Design, 2006) David Pearson, *The New Natural House Book: Creating a Healthy, Harmonious, and Ecologically Sound Home* (Fireside, 1998) Catherine Wanek, *The New Strawbale Home* (Gibbs Smith, 2003) B. C. Wolverton, *How to Grow Fresh Air: 50 House Plants That Purify Your Home or Office* (Penguin, 1997)